374

How to Plan and Manage an E-learning Progamme

How to Plan and Manage an E-learning Programme

ROGER LEWIS
and
QUENTIN WHITLOCK

GOWER

Published by
Gower Publishing Limited
Gower House
Croft Road
Aldershot
Hants GU11 3HR
England

Gower Publishing Company
Suite 420
101 Cherry Street
Burlington VT 05401–4405 USA

Roger Lewis and Quentin Whitlock have asserted their rights under the Copyright, Designs and Patents Act 1989 to be identified as the authors of this work.

British Library Cataloguing in Publication Data
Lewis Roger, 1944, Sept. 27-
    How to plan and manage an e-learning programme
    1. Education - Data processing 2. Training - Data processing
    I. Title II. Whitlock, Quentin A.
    370.2'85

ISBN 0566 08424 4

US Library of Congress Control Number: 2002106612

Typeset in 9 point Stone Serif by IML Typographers, Birkenhead, Merseyside and printed in Great Britain by MPG Books Limited, Bodmin, Cornwall

Contents

List of figures

List of tables

Introduction

E-learning is no longer new. It occupies a growing role in most education and training organizations. It is making the lives of individuals easier: helping people learn whilst at work or in the home, flexibly and at times that suit them. It is also meeting corporate objectives for cost -effective training and for introducing new procedures quickly. As technology and software improve, e-learning becomes faster, more reliable, more portable and easier to use. So, not surprisingly, e-learning is playing an increasing part in the lives of learners and of learning and training organizations.

It is no longer necessary to argue the case for e-learning. Clearly, not all programmes have proved successful and there is much that we can do to improve our uses of e-learning. As with earlier innovations (such as the video disk) the emphasis so far has been on content. The capacity of electronic media to store and transmit ever-increasing quantities of data has been exploited; more neglected has been the capacity of these media to help people communicate with one another and to share experiences. Such interaction between a learner and a tutor, or between learners themselves, is usually necessary for effective learning to take place.

E-learning has proved a dispiriting experience for some learners: slogging their way through unattractively presented content on a screen, unsure of where they are going and how long it will take to get there (if ever they arrive), aware only that it all seems to be taking a lot more time than they ever thought. Trainers using e-learning in this way are providing a one-way experience, focused on the needs of the provider rather than the user.

Excited by the technology, many educators and trainers seem to have forgotten some simple rules of good teaching. One of these is to focus on the learners. Who are they? What do they want/need to learn? Where will they be learning? What views are they likely to have on different ways of learning and new technologies? What help might they need – not just from computers but also from people?

Motivation to start learning, and to continue it, is as important with e-learning as with other media. Novel presentation methods and unfamiliar technologies can stimulate learners for a while but these attractions do not last long. Other sources of motivation are also needed and are longer lasting, such as the chance to talk to other learners, to an expert or to a trainer. Above all, people need the opportunity to check the effectiveness of their learning, by trying out new ideas and skills and getting feedback on their performance. These key conditions for learning may be met by electronic media but (depending on the programme) they may also require the intervention of tutors or trainers and the use of more traditional modes of learning, such as discussion groups, projects and seminars.

Designing attractive screens, with an intriguing use of visual and sound effects, is fine, but learners may be more motivated in the longer term by the chance to get credit for their learning. This may require liaison with a local college or university, which may prove more time-consuming than designing attractive screens but may be more important to the ultimate success of the programme.

A focus on the learner will open up other issues. There can be barriers both *to* using the technology and *in* using it. Some learners find it difficult to get access to electronic media. The obstacles may be physical (they simply don't have the necessary hardware) or psychological (they may be apprehensive about using the computer for learning). Once access is achieved there may then be other difficulties, such as the cost of telephone connection or of printing material from the screen; slowness and unreliability of operation; or issues of hardware compatibility.

Fortunately there are ways of addressing such problems. These include:

- analysing user needs, both at the corporate level (pay-offs for the sponsoring organization) and for individuals
- defining clear learning outcomes, to focus the learner's effort and to keep the content of the programme to a minimum
- designing assessment systems that test achievement of the outcomes and provide opportunities for learners to receive feedback
- producing clear and accurate explanations to learners of what the programme covers and how long it will take
- designing the programme flexibly, so not all learners need to study all parts
- using material that already exists, to reduce development costs
- using other media, for example print and audio, to reduce costs and introduce variety for learners
- using a tutor or trainer
- choosing a technological platform with the right combination of power, flexibility, affordability and ease of use
- providing a purpose-built environment for study.

There is nothing particularly new about these solutions. They apply to other forms of learning, whether innovative or not. But they are particularly important in e-learning, where learners may be dispersed and remote and where development costs can be high. These factors put a premium on careful planning.

The development of good e-learning programmes will usually require many different skills. Hence the importance of building a team, recruiting people with appropriate expertise and ensuring the team is properly supported.

Effective e-learning involves putting the needs of users at the centre of the development process – the needs of both sponsoring organizations and the learners. Good programme design also means getting feedback from users both during the development phase (for example through piloting) and when the programme is operating. Collecting and analysing such feedback, and modifying the programme accordingly, again requires careful planning and the allocation of time. But if these resources are not found, the quality of the programme cannot be assured.

What is this book about?

This book is for organizations wanting to make productive use of e-learning. The implications of adopting new learning strategies or delivery methods are far-reaching and usually require major developmental input. This applies to both education and training contexts.

The chapters of this book each explore an aspect of the effort needed to create the infrastructure for an e-learning initiative.

Chapters 1 and 2 comprise a step-by-step review of all the key stages in planning, implementing and managing an e-learning programme. We identify the decisions management must take at every stage and suggest strategies for monitoring, quality assurance, evaluation and revision of the programme. The remaining chapters amplify points introduced in these two chapters.

However well-designed, no e-learning programme will succeed unless business realities are addressed. These include establishing financial viability and a definition of the market(s) for the programme. Markets may be both internal and external. Chapter 3 explores the purposes of a business plan and helps the manager construct such a plan, including costing and marketing.

Electronic media offer ever more powerful means to reach learners. But the power of the media has to be harnessed by sound learning design. The next three chapters look at what is involved in this. Chapter 4 focuses on the analysis of the learning need: without this, the programme will lack purpose, promising what it cannot deliver. We consider three methods of arriving at a definition of learning need. Chapter 5 then shows how to identify outcomes for the learning programme, in terms of behaviour. It covers how to write sound outcomes and how to decide the ways in which these will be tested. With clear outcomes and assessment decided, the next stage is to analyse the programme content and skills, breaking this into manageable chunks and deciding on the learning sequence. Chapter 6 deals with these issues.

Assessment of learning merits a chapter of its own and Chapter 7 discusses assessment from the manager's point of view, including the various purposes of assessment, different types of test and when they are best used, and issues particular to assessment in e-learning.

In Chapters 8 and 9 we describe the closely related processes of creating learning materials and supporting the learners who use them. Some learning packages strive to be self-contained: they may include explanatory tutorials, worked examples, problems, questions and feedback, and all of these may be delivered online. Such so-called 'stand-alone courseware' is available in abundance from commercial suppliers and in-house development teams and can work for some people and for some subject matters – at least up to a point. However, experience in the UK over the past 30 years suggests that many, if not most, learners benefit from some form of tutorial support. This has always been a key principle in the Open University's provision; the Open Tech Programme and the Open College initiatives of the 1980s both came to the same conclusion; and the University for Industry's Learndirect programmes include tutorial support. So Chapter 8 describes how support for the e-learner can be provided, with particular reference to the role of tutors and mentors.

Materials design and development has recently been identified as a critical issue for managers of open and distance learning schemes whether in education or training. Standards of design and development are generally inadequate; developers are poorly trained, receive no accreditation and have low status. It makes sense wherever possible to use existing materials: you can save time and money by following the route set out in Chapter 9.

You will have to think hard about which media to use in your programme. People simply assume that e-learning means that all content is delivered on a computer screen. This is rarely adequate: it takes longer, and is more tiring to read from a screen than from a printed page, learners get bored with only one presentation method, and the learning outcomes often require a variety of media. Hence Chapter 10 explores the alternatives. It also covers the selection of development and delivery software for e-learning, the production of materials and how to establish an in-house learning centre.

A new e-learning scheme can have a powerful effect on an organization's tutors and trainers. They may love it or loathe it. It is clearly undesirable to trade on the enthusiasm of already hard-worked staff and in the long run this is likely to be counter-productive. An FE lecturer or company trainer will find it hard to 'fit in' e-learning design and tutoring alongside other more conventional teaching. The selection and training of e-learning staff, the conditions under which they do their work and their continuing professional development are all explored in Chapter 11, along with the advantages and disadvantages of carrying out work 'in house' or commissioning external bodies.

In Chapter 12 we treat a technical topic from the viewpoint of the e-learning manager: 'learning management systems'. We review the features and characteristics of a typical learning management system and discuss the implications for managers, authors and tutors. The chapter also deals with international standards, embracing apparently arcane matters such as 'learning object metadata'. The issue of standards is becoming increasingly significant and we aim to bridge the gap between the metadata metaphysicians and the manager seeking to ensure effective learning.

Finally, e-learning is full of specialist language and jargon. In the glossary at the end of the text we define the key terms we use in the book.

Acknowledgements

Several people helped us with this book.

A number of people read the manuscript and offered useful suggestions. The readers included Barbara Allan, Keith May and John Metcalf. Claire Bradley deserves special thanks as she read and commented on all the chapters.

We also received help with the illustrations. The screens from the histology programme in Chapter 12 (Learning management systems) were supplied by Dr Geoff Cope and Neil Everill of The University of Sheffield. The screens in Chapters 1, 5, 7, 8 and 12 from The Virtual Campus were supplied by Teknical; our thanks here go to Helmut Herberth and Tony Pedder. Finally the screen in Chapter 4 from the Capita system was provided by Sarah Wilkinson of Peak Dean Interactive.

1 *Planning an E-learning Programme: Part I*

CHAPTERS 1 AND 2 WILL HELP YOU:

- define the learners whose needs you intend to meet
- define what you expect your target group to learn
- describe the activities learners will carry out
- outline how learners will be assessed
- plan the learning programme.

Our starting point is that you want to design and operate a learning programme that uses e-learning for at least part of its delivery. You may choose to use other media as well: it does not always make sense to use electronic media for all purposes. Hence in this chapter we take a generic approach, to allow for a wide range of possible learning methods and delivery media.

We outline the things you will need to think about. Whether your programme is short or long, simple or complex, skills-based or more academic you will need to consider the points in the following checklist.

CHECKLIST: OVERVIEW QUESTIONS

Who are the learners?
What are they to learn?
How should the content be sequenced?
How can the content be broken down into 'chunks' manageable for learning?
What learning materials are needed? (In what media?)
What activities will learners take part in?
How will learners be assessed?
What tutorial and other support will learners need? Who will provide this? By what means?
How will learners access the support?
What resources will learners need access to?
What resources are available to you to develop the programme?

Thinking about each of these will trigger a lot of questions, such as:

- What learning materials already exist and can we use or adapt them?
- Do we need a full multi-media presentation? Can we afford it?
- Do our staff have enough experience of e-learning to prepare the programme?
- Will we be able to get learners together where the training need requires this?
- How can we get the programme running in six months?
- How can we persuade the learners to take part in electronic conferencing?
- Will employers be able and willing to support learners on projects?

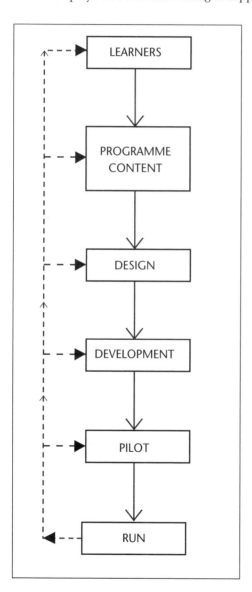

All these areas overlap and interact with each other. For example the learning materials you wish to use may require a particular type of tutorial support, or you may start with the activities learners will undertake and these will guide your decisions on other aspects of the programme.

You will almost certainly have to make some difficult decisions. For example you may want to use some existing learning material but it may be in an inappropriate format. Or the programme you want to design may be unsuitable for your learners or their circumstances. For example you may plan to deliver all materials and support online but your target audience may be mobile and prefer to use books and communicate by telephone; your assessment scheme may require group work but your learners may be unfamiliar with (or even hostile to) this form of assessment.

Figure 1.1 shows our proposed framework for developing an e-learning programme. You will see that we show a simple chronological sequence, from 'Learners' through to 'Run'. Any method of illustrating the process must acknowledge that stages overlap. Further, you will often have to reconsider a decision taken earlier in the process and perhaps change it. We have shown this by the dotted lines, running back up the sequence. Even though the framework has its limitations, it offers you a way to think systematically about planning. If you follow the stages of the framework, and the associated checklists, you should cover everything.

Figure 1.1   A framework for developing e-learning programmes

Go through this framework quickly. It will help you establish whether your programme is feasible. Can you deliver your plans? Have you the organizational capability, technical facilities and equipment, and resources? In later chapters we discuss these stages in more detail.

The learners: characteristics and context

Designers of learning are often tempted to start with content. But we recommend that you first consider the target audience: the learners (see Figure 1.2). This is even more important in e-learning than in conventional training. Good trainers can easily adjust their style and approach to the learners in front of them; in e-learning you have to communicate with learners whom you may never see. So you have to research your audience(s) fully in advance. However sound the content, if the presentation is unacceptable, the programme will fail.

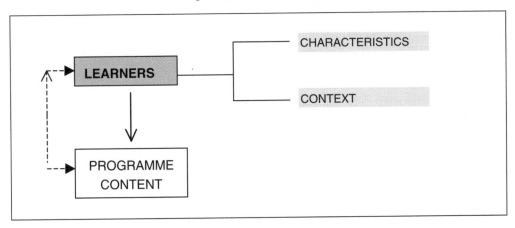

Figure 1.2   The learners

Considering your learner group will also lead to greater cost-effectiveness: the easier you make it for users to learn the fewer the demands they are likely to make on you. The better the learning tasks you design, the fewer questions learners will need to ask and the more likely they will be to complete the programme. Well-designed learning materials and appropriate technical platforms will help you avoid problems later.

You need to be clear as to who the learners are. Some programmes appeal to a wide audience; others are very specific. In a large organization, such as a bank or a government department, the learners may be numerous and drawn from a variety of social, educational and professional backgrounds. In other cases programmes may be targeted at a small and homogeneous group of employees with a particular skills need. The designer of the programme needs to understand the characteristics of the learning groups and the context in which they will be learning. Checklists for the kinds of points you should consider are set out below.

You should take into account any special physical characteristics needed by learners, for example visual acuity, agility or stamina. Keyboard skills, mouse usage and tolerance of screen glare may all warrant consideration. Previous educational background will influence programme design, for example the length of different modules, the style and level of language used and the use of illustrations. Motivation is also important: will learners want to undertake the programme? Will you need to help them through topics that they may perceive as less interesting or less relevant? Particular attitudes or prejudices might affect their approach to learning; these will influence the examples and illustrations you use. You will also need to take into account any distinguishing features of the trainees' work location, for example the type of customers they deal with or the layout of the office in which they work. Figure 1.3 shows a screen from a questionnaire to help participants in an online programme identify their preferred learning style.

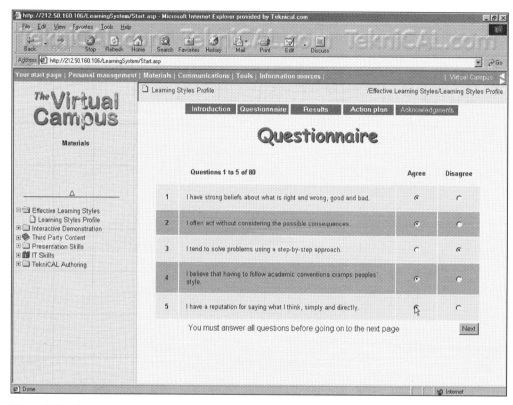

Figure 1.3   Questionnaire to determine learning style profile

---

CHECKLIST: LEARNER CHARACTERISTICS

Age
Physical characteristics
Likely confidence in learning new things
Likely level of skill in handling words, numbers, diagrams, equipment
Qualifications they already have
Learning methods with which they are familiar
Likely attitude to electronic learning
Motives for learning
Occupation
Cultural background and attitudes
Interests

CHECKLIST: LEARNER CONTEXT

Where will they learn? (At home? At work?)
How much time will they have for learning?
What equipment will they have (Hardware? Software? Network connection?)
When will they learn? (At night? During working hours?)
What are their family circumstances?
What difficulties may they experience (for example in gaining access to the necessary technology)?

One way we get programme designers to develop a clear picture of their learners is by asking them to sketch pen pictures. In design workshops we ask participants to construct a pen picture of a typical learner and includes details of age, location, family, motivation and previous experiences of learning.

This exercise can be repeated until several pen pictures are produced, giving a good 'feel' for the learners and their needs. From these, you can define the general characteristics, and also pinpoint any differences within the target group. Figure 1.4 is an example for an e-learning programme on managing cash-flow for small businesses.

Common points
Adults, mostly 25-50 years of age
Very limited time for study, say three–four hours each week
Short attention span; their focus will be on benefits to the business
Many distractions and other commitments (owners/managers of small businesses)
Need immediate application of their learning and speedy 'pay-offs'
Confident but likely to get impatient with 'academic' material
Likely to respond more positively to numbers/diagrams than to long prose passages
Access to computers at work and home; will want to learn in both places and at any time of day or night

Differences within the learner group
Varied educational background, from no qualifications to higher degrees
Not all will be used to 'modern' education/training methods
Diverse businesses (manufacturing/service and so on)
Varied interests/cultural backgrounds
Range of family circumstances
Equipment to which they have access will be varied in terms of power/specification

---

Figure 1.4   Target audience for a small business programme

This kind of analysis will help your planning. You might, for example, create a number of short modules to respond to users with different needs; you might use some printed materials to help users who want to learn whilst on the train or plane or wherever they don't have access to the computer.

Programme content: needs, outcomes, assessment and learning activities

As you can see from Figure 1.5, we use the term 'programme content' broadly, to include not only content in the traditional sense but also:

- the needs the programme wishes to meet
- the objectives learners will seek to achieve (the 'outcomes')
- the activities they will carry out to achieve the outcomes
- the means by which their performance will be assessed.

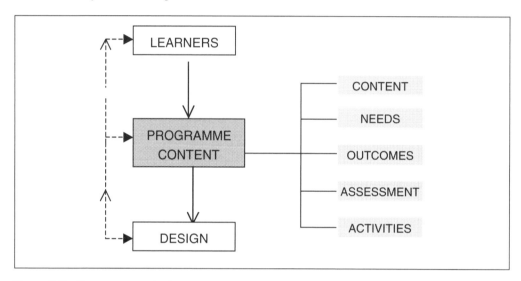

Figure 1.5   Programme content

These dimensions all interact: you can start with any one and it will inevitably lead you to the others. Some people find it easier first to work out the processes learners will experience (the learning activities); others begin with how they will recognize a successful learner (assessment); yet others with needs analysis. You will revisit the issues raised at this stage in more detail when you consider learning materials and any support structures you wish to provide or to stimulate.

CONTENT

You need to decide how you will select content. You could, for example, select by:

- analysing the outcomes you want learners to achieve
- looking at relevant competence tests/examinations/assessments
- considering the activities you want the learners to undertake
- reading reports prepared by quality reviewers, assessors or examiners
- looking at similar programmes
- brainstorming with colleagues, employers and other stakeholders.

Content and context

The treatment of content will depend to a large extent on the context in which the learning is to take place. For example some learning programmes are designed to help learners prepare for public examinations. These are more common in an FE/HE context. In a corporate context learning programmes are more likely to reflect the business plan of the organization and to assist employees in improving their performance.

Let us consider some of the issues that arise in selecting content in the context of a hypothetical example. The example is an induction course for new staff that has been run as a traditionally delivered training course. The programme is about to be adapted for online delivery. Hitherto the course has contained the following modules:

1 History of the company
2 An overview of our products
3 Company organization
4 Health & safety
5 Personal employment issues
6 Internal communications

The content of this programme, as in many others, will cover a range of different types of learning. These are some examples:

Theory	The products module includes an overview of the chemical laws concerning the process of converting oil to polymers
Concepts	The products module explains what polymers are
Procedures	The internal communications module explains how to use the company network to send e-mails
Physical skills	The health & safety module teaches how to dress a wound
Cognitive skills	The personal employment issues module explains how to interpret your pay slip

In its current form all those taking the induction course get the same content in the same sequence. As an e-learning programme the course will offer much more scope for individuals to access those parts of the content that they deem relevant to their personal needs. The designer of the e-learning programme will need to consider a number of questions:

• *Can the sequence be left entirely to choice or should some topics be taken in a fixed sequence?*

In this case sequencing can be left largely to the learner although certain key topics (for example security issues affecting movement about the works) will be marked for early attention.

• *Over what period should the learner study the content?*

Since this is an induction programme learners will be encouraged to complete it as soon as they can and, at the most, three months after their starting date in the organization.

• *How much enrichment material should be provided?*

Enrichment material comprises the 'nice to know' content that is not essential to the performance of a task but which some learners may find interesting. Links to such material can be inserted at the appropriate points within modules. Virtually the whole of Module 1 may be deemed to fall into this category. Several other modules such as 'An overview of our products' and 'Health & safety' will contain some 'nice to know' content.

- *Which parts of the programme lead to accreditation?*

It is not usual for an induction course to lead to accreditation but in this case the 'Health & Safety' module could well include an accredited unit for certain members of staff.

NEEDS

The content has to be relevant to the needs of the intended learners. These may be directly expressed by the learners themselves or arrived at by negotiation with other stakeholders. In corporate training, for example, the organization's business plan will suggest learning needs to be met. You may also have to consider the views of other stakeholders, for example a training board, professional body or awarding body.

Chapter 4 covers the analysis of needs in more detail. The process may be more or less complex, for example:

- you may be repackaging a conventional training course that already exists
- you may be meeting the requirements of an existing syllabus or competence framework
- you may be developing an entirely new programme.

There are a number of ways of determining training needs. Chapter 4 sets out three main approaches: performance analysis, goal analysis and surveys. As part of needs analysis you may need to:

- observe what employees actually do in their jobs (see the checklist below)
- interview employees about critical incidents in their job
- analyse customer complaints
- send a questionnaire to staff carrying out a particular operation.

CHECKLIST: OBSERVATION IN THE WORKPLACE

What procedures do experienced staff carry out?
What skills/knowledge do they need?
What aspects of the job do they find particularly difficult? Why?
What tools/equipment/machinery do they use?
What training do employees currently receive?

In Chapter 3 we discuss the way 'need' is turned into 'demand' through the process of marketing. You should, at the earliest planning stages, think about demand: will learners come to you direct or through another agency (for example, an employer)? How many learners do you expect? Who will be paying for the programme and how much will it cost? Such questions are at the heart of business planning, also covered in Chapter 3.

OUTCOMES

Your analysis of needs will help you to specify the kind of learning involved. This may, for example, be motor skills (such as operating equipment), intellectual (for example analysis of complex situations), attitudinal (such as developing confidence in new situations), interpersonal (for example communication, negotiation) – or it may be (and often is) some combination of these.

You will then be in a position to define outcomes – what the learners will be able to do as a result of the programme (also known as 'objectives'). You may first want to phrase these as an aim or goal before getting more specific, as in Figure 1.6.

Aim: to help learners define a project in the workplace

Outcomes
To draw up a specification for a workplace project, including outcomes, resources needed, timetable, method of assessment
To revise the specification as necessary, using feedback from a workplace mentor
To gain agreement to the project via a learning contract signed by tutor and workplace mentor

---

Figure 1.6   From aim to outcomes

Note that the *aim* is expressed in terms of the programme designer; the *outcomes* are what the learner will achieve and should be expressed in behavioural terms. We return to the translation of 'needs' into 'outcomes' in Chapter 5. At this stage your outcomes will be only initial; you will almost certainly need to modify them later.

ACTIVITIES AND LEARNING METHODS

Agreeing specific outcomes and how these will be assessed are the cornerstones of good learning design. They should determine the selection of content. Clarity over outcomes will also inform the choice of activities learners will carry out. These might include experiments, case studies and discussions.

The activities your learners engage in are crucial – through these they will learn. Do the activities require learners to:

- exchange information?
- work collaboratively?
- work in a real-time group?

The answers to such questions will help you to design the learning environment, both its physical components (any dedicated places in which learning occurs, such as learning centres) and the less tangible electronic learning spaces. A well-designed environment will help participants carry out the activities through which they will learn. You may need to be inventive: if, for example, the outcomes include skills needed to work with others you may have to find electronic equivalents to the activities learners would normally undertake face-to-face. Alternatively, you may need to include some provision for more traditional methods for experimenting and practising skills.

The activities you choose (sometimes called learning methods) will depend upon the type of learning involved and how it is to be assessed. If, for example, you are providing training in procedures, this may well best be delivered via the company's intranet. If you are developing interpersonal skills you may use role plays and simulations and occasional group face-to-face experiences. If you wish to assess learners' capacity to apply knowledge in the workplace, then projects may prove a good vehicle.

You should consider how much time learners will need to spend on the activities and test out your timings during piloting. Larger and more challenging activities will usually be broken into smaller components or stages. Realistic time allocations are a very important part of the learning environment: if you underestimate times learners can get very discouraged, finding they take much longer. Chapter 6 shows how you can break the necessary performance into sub-components, ready for assembling in a sequence that will make sense to the learner.

ASSESSMENT

At this early stage you will also need to think about how learners will be assessed. This usually has two aspects: 'end point' assessment (which may be linked to a qualification or a certificate to practise) and assessment along the way. There are different purposes behind the two kinds of assessment as in the example shown in Figure 1.7 (learning to drive a goods vehicle). The example also sets out the different characteristics of the assessment, flowing from the purpose, and who will use the results of the two types of assessment.

Type of assessment	Purpose	Characteristics	User(s)
On-going (formative)	To help the driver develop the necessary skills and knowledge	Informal; guides future learning; carried out by instructor; dialogue possible	Learner; instructor
Final (summative)	To license the candidate to drive certain classes of vehicle on public roads	Formal; carried out by (detached) examiner; little or no dialogue possible	Learner; instructor (for example to plan future instruction if necessary); government (in ensuring road safety)

Figure 1.7   Types of assessment and their consequences: learning to drive a goods vehicle

Responsibility for final assessment will depend on your context. Some examples are given in Figure 1.8. Whatever your responsibility for final assessment, you will certainly have a key role in designing ongoing assessment, because this is an essential part of the process of learning.

Responsibility for final assessment	Example	Implication for provider
External agency	Driving test	No direct involvement in final assessment
Part provider, part external agency	Much of GCSE assessment	Must understand and follow procedures set by external agency
Provider	Internal company skills test	Must design and implement final assessment

Figure 1.8   Responsibility for assessment

Assessment will show you, the learners and other stakeholders whether the outcomes have been achieved, and to what extent. So you need to think about the points in the checklist below.

CHECKLIST: ASSESSING YOUR LEARNERS

How will you assess?
What will you assess?
When will you assess?
Who will carry out the assessment?
What issues are involved (for example security, plagiarism)?

You may also want to consider how your learners may be helped to assess their own performance. This capacity is now generally regarded as important; amongst other things, it helps learners work independently of a tutor or trainer.

We return to assessment in Chapter 7.

Design

By now you should have a clear idea of the main thrust of your programme: who it's for, what needs it will meet, what you hope the users will learn and how you will assess that learning. This positions you well for the next stage: design (see Figure 1.9). This is largely about logistics: how the programme will be managed. It includes:

- the structure and length of the programme
- the sequencing of content and activities
- resources and constraints within which you must work
- how the programme will be delivered (how it reaches learners and is used by them).

STRUCTURE AND LENGTH OF THE PROGRAMME

Decisions here include:

- how the programme will be divided
- names and size of sub-parts (for example blocks, units, modules, sections)
- possible alternative routes through the material, to suit different learner needs.

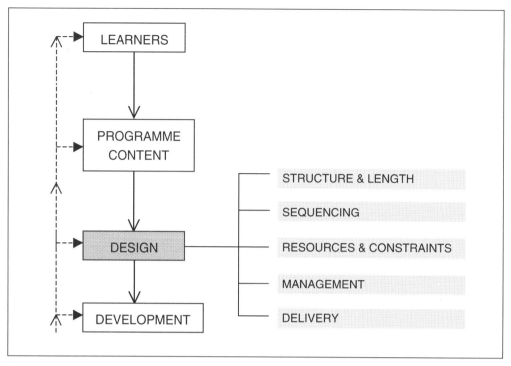

Figure 1.9   Programme design

Programme structures vary considerably, ranging from short 'stand-alone' updating units to elaborate programmes comprising several layers, occupying many learner hours and leading to a public qualification.

As with all aspects of programme planning we suggest you should always start from the perspective of the learner. You should think of structure in terms of hours of learning time. You need to make estimates in terms of an average learner. In the following example a 30-hour 'programme' is divided into three 'blocks' (see Figure 1.10).

The blocks are sub-divided into 'modules' of between one and three hours of learning time. The modules are further divided into sections of between 15 and 45 minutes. We have taken one module in one block to show the time breakdown of the various levels.

Other structural issues include:

- Will learners be able to start the programme at any time?
- Will learners be able to enter the programme at different starting points?
- Will learners be able to finish at any time?
- Will learners be able to navigate their own routes through the programme?
- Will there be pacing (for example, all learners have to reach a certain point at one time in order to be assessed)?
- Do you need to group learners together for particular activities or assessments?

Answers to these questions will depend upon your learners and your decisions on the issues raised earlier. Whenever possible you should give learners as much freedom as possible and cater for individual differences. Learners' circumstances often differ considerably: they may expect to start the programme whenever it suits them, and to work at their own speed. You

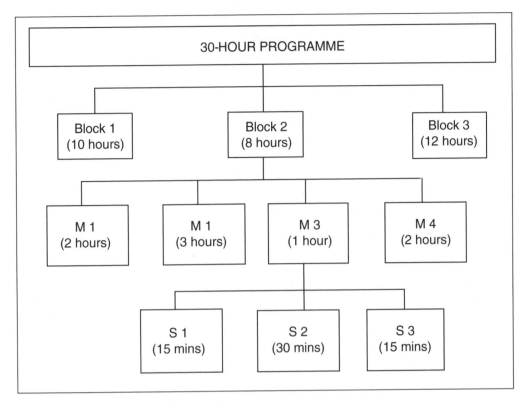

Figure 1.10   The structure and length of a programme

may, however, be operating under constraints that limit these freedoms. Experience also suggests that learners do need some degree of external discipline, for example a timetable that prompts them to work regularly: a number of online programmes require learners to submit assignments weekly or monthly. The media you choose may also impose constraints, for example electronic conferences may need to have a limited life.

SEQUENCING

You will have taken some decisions earlier about programme content. You now need to work further on this, for example deciding how topics may best be sequenced. This links to decisions about programme structure. You will need to decide, for example, which topics are sufficiently 'stand-alone' to be treated separately.

You can tackle sequencing in a number of different ways:

- by chronological order or dependency (this topic needs to be learned before that topic)
- by motivation (this topic is more interesting than that topic so we'd better start with it)
- by level of difficulty (we'll start with the easier topics).

You may choose to focus on problems or case studies that raise central issues. Or you may wish to use a 'spiral' approach, whereby the learner returns several times to key content, but at increasing levels of complexity.

You may wish to provide alternative pathways through the programme, for example to support learners who have difficulties or those who wish to omit certain sections. In this case, you may need to provide a diagnostic test or other means by which learners can choose their own routes through the programme. We go into more detail on sequencing in Chapter 6.

RESOURCES AND CONSTRAINTS

Whatever your situation, you will have to work with the resources you have available, respecting any constraints. Resources come in a number of forms: people, time, learning materials, equipment, expertise, budgets, buildings. Some of these will be directly accessible to you (for example staff in your organization who report to you); others less accessible (for example a network of employers who may offer facilities). You should carry out an audit of what you have available – and of any gaps. If these gaps are critical you need to consider how you will fill them; for example if you have no in-house authors you may be able to commission a freelance writer, or form a partnership with another organization. (We discuss these issues in Chapter 11.) Constraints regularly encountered include:

- limited knowledge of the topic within the organization
- job/task instability (subject to changes)
- lack of development time
- lack of experience of learning design
- conflicting management imperatives and decisions
- lack of opportunities for learners to practise (for example on expensive or heavily used equipment)
- printer and network problems
- the limits of the learning platform within which you have to work
- inflexible systems administrators
- lack of skilled authors or tutors.

You need particularly to consider the technological infrastructure required to achieve your programme plans, as in the checklist below.

CHECKLIST: THE TECHNOLOGY

Does your system need to be integrated into the Web?

What learning platform or conferencing system will you use? Will you need to customize it?

What electronic facilities do you need to make available to your learners, for example to take part in conferencing?

What additional facilities will tutors need, for example to control conferences?

How will these facilities relate to your existing systems (for example e-mail systems)?

How many learners/tutors will the system need to support, both now and in the foreseeable future?

Will you need to distribute software to learners? If so, how?

Will learners be using the equipment in their homes? If so, what equipment specification will they need?

What on-going technical support will you provide, for exmple upgrading, helpline?

What specification will be needed for this support? Where, how and when will it be accessed?

MANAGEMENT

Whatever the nature of your scheme you will have to ensure it functions smoothly. You will need to cover some or all of the following management and administrative tasks.

CHECKLIST: MANAGEMENT

Marketing
Recruitment and enrolment
Receipt of fees
Making payments (for example to suppliers, tutors)
Maintenance of network and other IT systems and services
Updating of learning materials

We say more about these points in our discussion of learning management systems in Chapter 12.

DELIVERY

Delivery refers to the way in which your programme reaches the learner. You will usually have to consider two aspects: the learning material and additional support, such as assessment, guidance and technical support. 'Delivery' isn't a particularly satisfactory term: you cannot 'deliver' learning like a newspaper or a parcel. Learning requires a participant at the other end – whose activity is essential for learning to take place. Nevertheless, since delivery is such a common term, we use it here.

Delivery of learning material

First, then, the learning material. Most programmes include a body of content; in addition, good learning material also incorporates advice, guidance, testing, feedback – all of which help the individual remain active and learn. (You will note the grey area between 'learning material' and 'support': these features of the material are supporting student learning.)

The learning material can sometimes be considerable in size – for example if the programme is ambitious in scope or if the subject matter requires the understanding and application of an extensive body of knowledge. You may decide that print is the most appropriate medium; it is generally not good practice to use electronic media to broadcast inert information.

You will need to think about how best to get the learner to interact with the content of the programme. There are a number of potential media: electronic, print, audio, video, real objects (such as particular equipment or raw material). Each has its strengths and weaknesses. Electronic media are particularly effective at supporting interaction between learners and group working.

You will need to consider not only your own needs but also those of the learner. We start by practising what we preach, and take the learner first (Figure 1.11).

Medium	Advantage to learner	Disadvantage to learner
Electronic	Can print off only what they need	Can be difficult to read from a screen; printing can be expensive; equipment is needed; not easily portable
Print	Easily portable; the pages are often bound rather than loose	Long texts can be intimidating
Audio cassette	Convenient for use when in the car or on the move	Can be difficult to maintain concentration for long periods
Video cassette	Can be motivating	Requires equipment; not portable

Figure 1.11   Media from the learner's perspective

You will need to give particular attention to the technology learners will use, the costs associated with it (including the costs of supporting the equipment in use) and who pays these costs. Much will depend on the context in which learners are accessing electronic media. Will they be using it at home? At work? In a learning centre? In several places? If different learner groups have differential access (and incur different costs) you may need to select technology that is inexpensive, unsophisticated and easy to use and support.

Figure 1.12 takes your perspective, as provider. An important point emerges here: what

Medium	Advantage to learner	Disadvantage to provider
Electronic	Eliminates printing/duplication costs; easily reaches large and/or dispersed numbers	Certain types of audio-visual presentation can be time-consuming to design and require high performance machines
Print	Proven technology	Costs of printing and delivery (for example postal charges)
Audio	Inexpensive to produce and duplicate	Updating, storage and distribution costs
Video	If the programme has a strong visual element this can be more economical than on-screen graphics	Can be expensive to shoot a video of a good standard; updating, storage and distribution costs

Figure 1.12   Media as seen by the provider

might be good from a provider's point of view may not suit a learner. A good example is the sole use of electronic media to communicate learning material. If this is extensive the learner will find it hard to handle all the information on screen. They will thus need to print it off. This transfers costs (of printing, collating and 'binding') from producer to learner.

Some media are more complex than others to deliver. The complexity can be located either at the production/distribution end or at the learners' end. Print, for example, is easy for learners to use and handle. They simply get it in the post or buy it from a bookshop; they can carry it around with them, using it easily in a variety of places. But print may not be convenient for a manager, who has to develop a system for printing, collating, binding, stocking and despatching the product. Software is, in contrast, much simpler for the provider to input, store, update and transmit – but, as we have seen, it might impose constraints on the learner.

Much will depend on the circumstances of you the provider and of your learners. If, for example, you already have in place staff and systems for printed publication then you may be able to use these for the learning material at marginal extra cost. Or you may be able to 'buy in' a printed resource without having to publish it yourself, for example you might incorporate a published book into your programme. Similarly, if your target audience has easy access to computers, printers and other equipment at work, and their employer is happy for these to be used for learning, then delivery of the material by electronic means might make good sense.

You need to consider the learner's motivation. There is a lot of evidence to suggest that most learners like variety. They get bored with any medium, however convenient and powerful it may be, if it is used for long periods. They like a change. Many successful programmes consciously use a variety of media. This not only stimulates the learner but also caters for different approaches to learning: some individuals learn through listening, others prefer visual routes, yet others prefer to learn by reading. A variety of media can also support remedial or extension learning. We return to media selection in Chapter 10.

Delivery of support

A programme will usually deliver not only learning material but also other forms of support. These may include orientation/induction, feedback, routine contact, the facility to have questions answered, practical experience, tuition, help in emergencies. Guidance on assessment, including the tasks and criteria used to judge performance, is essential.

Such guidance is sometimes made available in a 'programme guide', together with information on expected outcomes, learning methods, content and advice on how to use the various programme components.

These forms of support have traditionally been delivered by a variety of media, including face-to-face, post and telephone. It is possible to use just one medium for all purposes. In old style correspondence education, for example, post was the single medium. Currently some programmes use only electronic means to orchestrate a wide range of contacts of different kinds between learners and with their tutor. Or (and more commonly) several media can be used in conjunction, as for example with the Open University, where students can often choose between post, telephone, face-to-face and electronic media.

Again, you can decide to locate the complexity at the provider's end or at the learner's end. Traditionally, for example, colleges and training centres are good at providing face-to-face support. They are equipped for this and their staff are experienced at it. But attending a fixed place at a fixed time can be inconvenient for learners, especially if they have other commitments or spend a lot of time travelling. Hence the growth of other means of providing support, such as electronic media. As with the learning material, a mix of delivery methods for support is often popular with students but this kind of provision will obviously be more expensive and you (or the learners) may not be able to afford it.

The checklist below will help you consider key points about delivery. We discuss managing learner support in Chapter 8.

CHECKLIST: DELIVERY

What are your learners' likely media preferences: for the materials, for support?

What learner needs must your system meet? (For example need to leave messages, get responses within a set time, receive support outside 'office hours')

How can you meet the learners' preferences with the resources you have available?

Will electronic media on their own be sufficient to deliver (a) the material, (b) other support?

Will special premises be necessary, for example for running tutorials and/or for private study?

Have you considered all the costs to *the learner*? (Include telephone costs, internet access, printing costs, travel costs, equipment costs)

Have you considered all the costs *you* will have to meet? (For example in setting up assessment systems, paying tutors, maintaining electronic networks)

Will learners need access to special experiences? (For example to carry out projects, to gain 'hands-on' experience of operating equipment; to develop interpersonal skills)

Are your delivery systems likely to prove reliable? Flexible? Will they promote interactivity?

Conclusions

We have reached the end of the discussion of the design stage. We said earlier that our model is an iterative one, that is you need to double back every so often to review the decisions you provisionally took earlier. Our philosophy is that the learner should always be placed at the heart of programme planning. So now would be a good time to look again at your earlier analysis of the learners and the learning. In the light of that reappraisal you may decide that certain design elements are essential. Some examples are given in Figure 1.13.

Now you have looked at the broad design of your programme you need to make specific provision for three main elements: learning materials, learner support and management. These are the main working components of any e-learning programme and they interact. We consider these in the next chapter.

Learner characteristic	Implication for design
Used to working to a timetable	Schedule regular assignments; issue automatic reminders
Need assurance that what they are learning is relevant to their job	Provide a workplace mentor; use work-based projects for assessment
Lack confidence in learning	Build learning skills development into materials; brief mentors on this topic
Want to start the programme when it suits their timetable	Register learners at any time in year; provide 'on demand' inductions
Want to develop a series of separate skills	Produce short, self-contained modules
Want a qualification	Negotiate with awarding/examining bodies

Figure 1.13   Learner-centred design

SUMMARY

In this chapter we have covered the first three stages of planning:

- analysis of the learner group: the characteristics of the learners and the context in which they are taking the programme
- content of the programme: what has to be learned, managing stakeholder needs, assessment of learning
- design: length and structure of the programme, sequencing of learning, resources and constraints, management and delivery.

2 *Planning an E-learning Programme: Part II*

CHAPTER 2 WILL HELP YOU:

- decide what kinds of learning materials you will need and what additional tutorial (or other) support will accompany them
- plan how you will pilot or test the programme and amend it in the light of feedback
- plan how you will monitor your course once it is running and modify it as necessary
- decide what arrangements you will make for quality assurance.

In the previous chapter we looked at the first three stages of the planning process:

- analysis of the learner group
- programme content
- design.

In this chapter we discuss the final three stages:

- develop
- pilot
- run.

Develop

The design stage will have helped you identify how you will meet learner needs within the resources available to you. If the solution is an e-learning programme you will need to consider how you will develop the necessary learning materials and associated support. This will inevitably raise some management issues.

We look in detail at the three main elements of an e-learning programme: learning materials, support and management (Figure 2.1) – in later chapters. Here we give introductory checklists of the kinds of things you need to consider at the planning stage together with an indication of where you can find more extensive coverage.

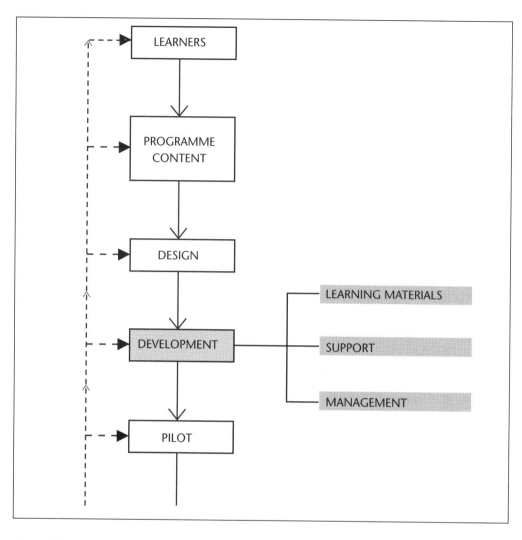

Figure 2.1   Development

CHECKLIST: LEARNING MATERIALS (SEE CHAPTERS 9 AND 10)

What criteria do you want the learning material to meet? (Include content, medium, style)

How quickly do you need to begin the training?

What learning material already exists? Has this been evaluated/tested?

Is existing material suitable (a) as it stands, (b) if you adapt it?

Do you need to produce your own material? Do you need to sub-contract production?

By what criteria will you monitor the effectiveness of the learning material?

What monitoring methods will you use?

How frequently will you update the material?

CHECKLIST: SUPPORT (SEE CHAPTER 8)

What support (additional to the learning material) will learners need?

Will learners need induction to the programme (for example preparatory materials, a briefing)?

How much support will learners be entitled to receive (for example in terms of frequency and duration)?

Will learners need technical support (for example to resolve systems problems)?

Will support be provided entirely by electronic means? Which other methods might you use (for example post, telephone)?

Who is best placed to support the learner (for example a tutor, fellow learners, colleagues at work, a work mentor)?

What skills will the supporter need?

How will you choose, train and motivate any supporters involved?

Will a partnership/collaboration with another organization (for example a college or company) add value?

By what criteria will you monitor the effectiveness of the support?

What monitoring methods will you use?

CHECKLIST: MANAGEMENT

What is the business plan for the programme? (See Chapter 3)

What arrangements will you make for marketing the programme? (See Chapter 3)

How will management responsibilities for all major activities be allocated? (Include budgetary maintenance, time allocation of individuals/teams, progress chasing and monitoring standards)

What arrangements will you make for selecting, inducting, training and monitoring staff? (See Chapter 11)

These three elements – materials, support and management – are dynamically related. They should be co-ordinated to meet learner requirements. We can extend parts of our earlier example (see Figure 1.13) to show how this may be achieved (Figure 2.2).

Pilot

The development phase is likely to take some time; the processes relating particularly to learning materials can take several months, even for a limited programme. You will then be ready to move ahead – but we suggest you proceed to a pilot stage (Figure 2.3) rather than to full operation. By a 'pilot' we mean offering the programme, or a coherent part of it, to a sample group of learners. Even 10 to 20 would be enough. This is particularly important when you are developing your own learning materials, to ensure the style, tone and level of difficulty are suitable. This can avoid lengthy and costly adaptations later on.

Learner characteristic	Implication for design	Implication for development
Used to working to a timetable	A structured programme: regular assignments; automatic reminders	*Materials*: publish assignments and deadlines in advance *Support*: tutors to reinforce deadlines *Management*: include assignment dates in programme regulations
Need assurance that what they are learning is relevant to their job	Provide a workplace mentor, use work-based projects for assessment	*Materials*: produce mentor guidelines *Support*: select and train workplace mentors *Management*: negotiate mentoring arrangements with employers

Figure 2.2   Learner-centred development

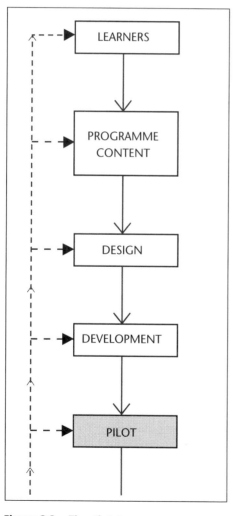

You may need to offer incentives to persuade learners to take part in the pilot. These might include the opportunity to gain credits towards a qualification, or a significant reduction in course fees. In the corporate context you may also need to gain the support of line managers, for example to release their staff.

A pilot will enable you to try out the main elements of your programme and get feedback from your target learner group(s). You can then revise the programme before it 'goes live'. (Some people use the term 'developmental test', 'field test' or 'validation' instead of 'pilot'.)

You need to identify any issues on which you particularly need feedback, especially those relating to the learning materials and support.

Figure 2.3   The pilot stage

CHECKLIST: PILOTING

Have you identified a representative learner group?
Have you decided how to brief the pilot learners?
Have you planned a realistic timescale for the pilot?
Have you decided what data to collect, how you will collect it and how you will analyze it?
Have you allowed time to adapt your programme in the light of feedback from the pilot?

Run

After the pilot, and any modifications to the materials or support arrangements, you are ready to run the programme (Figure 2.4). Once running, you need to monitor how it all works. In particular you need to:

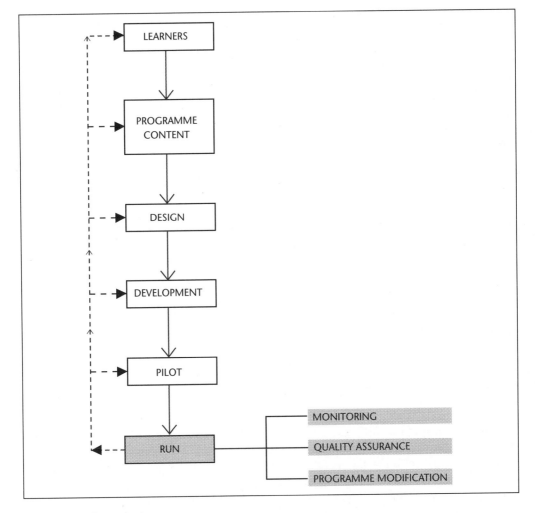

Figure 2.4   The operation stage

- identify critical activities
- set standards for these activities
- identify information that will help you check if the standards are being met
- analyse the data
- act accordingly.

Areas for monitoring should reflect your analysis of learners/learning. For example if you decided that your learners need helpful tutors, relevance to work and employer help with projects then you would need to make sure that these are being provided. Activities you might need to monitor could include:

- marketing
- efficiency of registering learners onto the programme
- student perceptions of the learning material
- length of time learners take to study different modules
- learner achievement rates
- programme completion rates
- quality of tutor feedback to students.

Figure 2.5 gives some examples of standards (measures of effectiveness) that might be set for some of these activities.

Activities	Standard
Marketing	Enquiries coming equally from all departments within the company Advertising in company newsletter/on intranet to generate minimum of 50 enquiries
Perceptions of the learning material	Minimum of 75 per cent of learners find the material attractive/very attractive Maximum of 25 per cent of learners find the material difficult/very difficult
Learner completion rates	A minimum of 65 per cent of learners complete the programme
Tutor feedback	Tutors respond to learner questions and assessments within seven days

Figure 2.5   Examples of standards

You then need to identify the information that will help you decide if the standard is being met. Figure 2.6 extends our earlier example to show possible sources of information.

No one source of information will tell you all you need to know: you will also need to consult a variety of other sources. You may, for example, need to interview learners or tutors, to help you interpret information you may have collected electronically.

The information you collect will not be self-evident: it will need analysis. For example

Activities	Standard	Source of information
Marketing	Enquiries coming equally from all departments within the company Advertising in company newsletter to generate minimum of 50 enquiries	Enquiry log
Perceptions of the learning material	Minimum of 75 per cent of learners find the material attractive/very attractive Maximum of 25% of learners find the material difficult/very difficult	Completed questionnaires
Learner completion rates	A minimum of 65% of learners complete the programme	Learner log-on rates for essential assessments
Tutor feedback	Tutors should respond to learner questions and assessments within seven days	E-mail exchanges Log of receipt/marking of assessments

Figure 2.6 Sources of information

only 20 enquiries may have been generated through the company newsletter but if its publication was delayed then this information will be inconclusive. After analysing the information you then need to act accordingly. Examples of moving from analysis to action are given in Figure 2.7.

Activity	Issue raised by analysis of information	Action
Marketing	Enquiries generated from advertising are well below the standard; word of mouth is the most effective medium	Revise marketing budget to support successful media and reduce/eliminate unsuccessful
Learning material	A significant minority of learners find the cartoons irritating	Develop a different style of illustration
Completion rates	Only 30 per cent of learners in Company A complete the course	Interview Company A learners to establish causes of drop-out; draw up action plan and discuss this with the sponsor
Tutor feedback	Tutor B consistently fails to meet the deadline for responding to student e-mails	Contact Tutor B to establish whether (s)he wishes to continue tutoring and can meet quality standards

Figure 2.7 Moving from analysis to action

You will also need to ensure that responsibility for action is clear and agreed. Who takes action? By when? With what resources? Responsibility may lie with:

• you as programme manager
• an administrator
• an editor
• a programme team
• tutors or mentors.

You will want to concentrate your effort on areas in which standards are not being met. Sometimes a standard may be exceeded. For example 80 per cent of learners instead of the 75 per cent target may find the material attractive/very attractive. Here you may decide to raise the standard.

You will see from the preceding discussion that monitoring covers activities under the three major elements we described earlier: learning materials, support and management. Another way of viewing monitoring is that it can operate at a number of levels, for example the whole programme or sub-sections of a programme; all tutors, a sub-set of tutors or an individual tutor; all learners a sub-set of learners, or an individual learner.

QUALITY ASSURANCE

We have already covered some aspects of quality assurance: setting standards, monitoring performance against these standards and taking corrective action as necessary. Readers in higher or further education have to operate within another set of processes, those set and audited by or on behalf of a funding body. These are largely about the processes education providers use to assure the quality of their programmes.

If you work in training and development within public or private sector organizations you are more likely to be familiar with the International standard ISO9000. To gain certification under this standard you need to:

• identify key business processes (for example registering learners, preparing materials)
• describe how these processes should be carried out (via 'procedures' and more detailed 'work instructions')
• establish an audit system for checking that the procedures are carried out
• develop a 'corrective action procedure' for putting right, and learning from, failures to follow the procedures
• review the system and develop it as necessary.

Some organizations have used this process to assure the quality of the development and production of learning material.

Your organization may prefer to view quality assurance as part of 'total quality management' (or another holistic term to indicate a pervasive approach to quality by all employees, rather than a codified system). In this case, you will continually be asking of a process 'How can we do this better?'

Or you may choose to put together your own approach to quality, using parts of different approaches that meet your own needs. Our own approach to quality assurance is shown in the previous section: setting standards, monitoring performance and seeking constantly to improve.

SUMMARY

In this chapter we have worked through the key stages of planning an e-learning programme. Some points are specific to training and e-learning; others relate more generally to the planning of *any* project, for example:

- defining each task to be carried out, with its output
- breaking down each task into component activities
- identifying any dependencies (tasks that have to be carried out before others)
- setting start and end dates for each activity
- allocating responsibilities for each task, together with the time allowed
- identifying resources needed.

It is good practice to set measures of success for each activity, check that these are being achieved and to take action if necessary.

3 Business Planning and Marketing

THIS CHAPTER WILL HELP YOU:

- describe the chief purposes of a business plan for e-learning
- identify the main components of a business plan
- construct a business plan appropriate to your context
- develop a marketing plan.

The expression 'business plan' has become widely used in recent years. When it first gained currency about twenty years ago the term denoted a financial forecast, typically drawn up by a new business, to meet a bank`s condition for a loan or overdraft. While the financial element is still central to a business plan, the document now tends to contain a much wider range of information, including a detailed product description and objectives. The plan may also be required for many other purposes than simply a bank loan, for example as part of a feasibility project for a new programme.

Many publications explain the detailed procedures of business planning (Cohen 1994). In this chapter we aim to help those new to the management of e-learning projects to identify the key elements, particularly those relating to the financial implications of their planning, such as costing, pricing and budgeting. These will be different from the structures of conventional education or training.

As recently as three or four years ago online models of e-learning were regarded as experimental, futuristic or freakish. This is no longer the case. While it would be premature to use the word 'commonplace', a variety of models of online learning are established in both the education and the corporate sectors. Indeed in the latter case enough progress has been made to warrant the publication by the Department of Trade & Industry of a report comprising 12 case studies of large scale business applications of e-learning (DTI 2000). As the Secretary of State wrote in the foreword to this publication: 'On-line delivery of learning, often supported by coaching and mentoring, is increasingly becoming the norm.' A similar advance has been made in the education sector, although the models that are evolving there are often very different from the business applications.

These initiatives have generated a variety of 'best practice' guidelines that will certainly help the company, college or university starting out on the online learning trail to avoid the obstacles that tripped up the earliest practitioners.

Purposes of the business plan

A sound business plan enables the e-learning champion to achieve a number of goals. First, it helps to promote the scheme: in reviewing benefits and constraints the business plan helps make the case to both management and end users. As we explain in a later chapter, selling the scheme is as important as devising it. Thus the business plan will be an essential precursor to the orientation programme that should introduce e-learning to all the stakeholders.

Second, a business plan will help determine costs and benefits of the programme. The plan may also make a case for development funding, for example for learning materials and evaluation.

Third the business plan will be the starting point for the more detailed project management plan necessary to achieve the programme's objectives.

ELEMENTS OF THE BUSINESS PLAN

Figure 3.1 sets out the main elements of a typical business plan for e-learning. We cover each of these in turn.

Scope of the project	The aim of the project and how it relates to other corporate objectives
Review of expected benefits	The main benefits accruing to the learners and other stake-holders
Description of the programme	The titles and outcomes of learning modules, the format and the delivery mode
Financial forecast	Income and expenditure expected over the life of the project (including start-up costs and other resources needed, such as staffing and equipment)
Marketing plan	A description of the market/s, end users, promotional methods, pricing strategy and so on.

Figure 3.1   Elements of the business plan

The emphasis placed on these elements will vary according to the nature of the organization. There is an obvious difference in scope between an educational institution and a business corporation. A university may be attended by 20 000 full-time students and employ 2000 academic staff. Undergraduates are enrolled in cohorts. It will be quite common for groups of 60 or 100 undergraduates to take the same programme simultaneously. By contrast company training and educational applications will tend to address a far wider range of requirements. The need will undoubtedly arise to distribute the same materials to hundreds of staff in different locations, for example when a new computer system is to be adopted. But it is just as likely that some materials will need to be studied by only a few individuals. Some businesses will buy generic packages off-the-shelf to help particular individuals learn specific skills when they are needed, such as computer-based bookkeeping or time management.

Another factor that may affect the emphasis within the business plan will be the previous experience of open and distance learning within the organization. In some cases there will be no previous history of this. In others the organization will be introducing online learning as a natural successor to existing print-based and computer-based applications. In the latter instance the need to 'sell' the new methodology is likely to be less compelling.

The approach to costing will also vary between organizations. Some educational institutions will expect programme development and delivery costs to be fully recovered from fees. In others the cost recovery principle will not apply and online students will be treated on the same basis as those learning by other methods. Within a corporate context there may be notional transactions between departmental budgets or the whole development and operation of the programme may be funded from the organization's training budget.

The business plan will often be prepared in a series of stages. You might make the initial plan some months before start-up and revise it closer to the start-up date as more details become available. In the light of your first running of the online programme you will revise the plan again. Indeed within a large organization the whole process might be conducted over a period as long as three to five years.

The business plan will need to be accompanied by other plans related to the development of the programme. Each of these will be relevant to a particular user or users. Examples are given in Figure 3.2.

Plan type	User(s)
Training specification	Authors, editors
Production plan	Programmers, project manager
Delivery plan	Project manager for tutorial support

Figure 3.2   Related plans and their users

A business plan for an e-learning programme would also need to fit with other organizational plans; we turn to this next.

Scope of the project

Of course the business plan made by e-learning managers – whether they are working in a business or an academic context – will not be the only business plan in use within the organization. There will almost certainly be a corporate plan with an accompanying set of strategy documents, one of which might cover training and development. Companies that set up e-learning schemes, particularly those on a larger scale that may be called virtual universities, stress the need for these to be integrated into the broader corporate plan. A Henley Management College publication makes the point: 'a corporate university is formed when a corporation seeks to relate its training and development strategies to its business strategy by coordination and integration and by the development of intellectual capital within the organisation in pursuit of its corporate aims' (Henley Management College 2000).

Thus the starting point for the e-learning business plan must be to show how it will help the organization meet its wider strategic goals.

The report on *The Future of Corporate Learning* (DTI 2000) raises a number of issues that the business planner may need to review in scoping the business plan:

- How does your structure add value to the business strategy?
- Who will champion your scheme?
- How will staff be involved?
- What existing provision can be built on?
- How will learning be delivered?
- What will be the role of managers and trainers in delivering and supporting learning?
- How will learning be promoted?
- Is learning accredited?

A business plan taking these factors into account is more likely to attract management interest than one that focuses merely on the technical aspects of the e-learning programme.

Benefits of e-learning

Most business plans will include a description of the expected benefits of the e-learning scheme. The practical benefits fall under four headings:

1 New markets
2 Economic benefits
3 Added value partnerships
4 Enhanced learning outcomes

NEW MARKETS

E-learning programmes can access new markets in three ways:

- widening geographical coverage for programmes
- developing new products
- opening access to new learner groups.

Wider geographical coverage

The geographical possibilities for e-learning are literally worldwide. In the higher education sector the numbers of universities offering some form of e-learning opportunity to overseas students has increased exponentially in the past five years. Business administration is a good example. The 1997/98 Directory of MBAs lists the Open University in the UK and two universities in the USA (Phoenix and ISIM) as offering MBAs by distance learning. At the start of 2001 the MBA Info Web site listed 288 MBA programmes at 199 establishments! In a different way large corporations also use e-learning to reach their staff in overseas locations. New e-universities run by such companies as Unisys, Unipart, Motorola and BA are all accessible by thousands of students – in some cases tens of thousands – worldwide.

New product development

Experience in both education and corporate sectors demonstrates that e-learning can stimulate the development of new products. The phenomenal growth in online MBA delivery is probably exceptional but many other examples can be found in both academic and business applications. Some new products developed within the corporate e-universities described in the DTI report are distributed on a very wide scale. In the further education sector the Learning to Teach On-Line (LeTTOL) course run by the South Yorkshire Further Education Consortium is one of the most successful online courses in the UK. LeTTOL was an entirely new product; both its subject-matter and its delivery mode were online learning. An example of new product development in the business sector is M&G's I university which has developed a 20-hour online course on equities.

Access to new types of learner

Almost every organization using e-learning finds that it attracts new categories of participant. In some cases this is a by-product of the initiative. In others it is a deliberate strategy from the outset. An example of the latter case is the University for Industry (UfI) in the UK, which uses e-learning in its Learndirect learning centres to attract social groups in the post-16 age range that hitherto have avoided new learning experiences. By the end of 2000 over 400 courses were available at over 700 Learndirect centres, 87 per cent of which were online. In the USA a National Education Association poll of distance learning tutors (reporting in November 2000) found that staff teaching both distance learning and traditional courses: 'hold positive opinions about distance learning ... because [it] offers educational opportunities to students who would not otherwise enrol in courses' (www.nea.org/he).

ECONOMIC BENEFITS

The cases we have cited show that e-learning can be economically viable. In the UK the LeTTOL course more than covers its costs. The University of British Columbia's (UBC) experience was that on-line courses, especially when developed through partnerships, can be cost recoverable or at least as cost effective as conventional courses. (Bartolic-Zlomislic and Bates n.d.). The UBC programme itself made a profit. The upfront costs are high, especially if you are developing materials from scratch that have to be largely self-contained. On the other hand, while the development costs may appear high to management, they can be spread over time and partners can share the costs.

Corporate experience reflects that of UBC. A comprehensive cost–benefit study by Bell Canada (Whalen and Wright 2000) reports the findings on two courses that echo many other corporate e-learning ventures:

- A two-and-a-half hour asynchronous course with a short video, using WebCT software, took 1487 hours to develop. It had a five-year return on investment of 288 per cent – for every $1 Bell spent it saved $3. The break-even point came after the first 111 students used the course.
- A four-hour synchronous course using Astra's symposium software took 144 hours to develop and had a five-year return on investment of 3283 per cent. Bell saved $33 for every $1 spent. Payback came after the first four students had used the course.

As with other forms of open and distance learning, e-learning can be strikingly cost-effective in the corporate context: 'undeniably, e-learning cuts the costs of travel, facilities, administrative overheads, duplication of effort and most importantly the opportunity cost of people away from the job' (the e-learning FAQ <www.internettime.com>).

Paul Fox has devised this simple formula for calculating the return on investment (ROI) of e-learning schemes (www.foxperformance.com):

$$ROI = \frac{Benefits - costs}{Costs} \times 100$$

If you determine that the benefits of a programme or consulting intervention are $20 000 and the costs of the programme were $5000 this gives you:

$$ROI = (20\,000 - 5000) = \frac{15\,000}{5000} = 3 \times 100 = 300\%$$

A well-documented case study on ROI is the Logistics End User Computing Enabler Project (LEUCIE) undertaken by the Intel corporation and reported in 2000 (www.learningtopics.com/ROICaseStudy.htm). This is an electronic performance support system (EPSS) supporting a new report generating application. The system includes embedded e-learning of 1–2 hours duration, replacing 8–12 hours of classroom training. In addition users have 24 hours a day access to the other support features: reference information, step-by-step cards and simulations. Use of LEUCIE is tracked automatically through the networks on which it is installed. This enables the ROI calculation to be computed with a good degree of accuracy.

PARTNERSHIPS

As we have seen, a remarkable number of successful e-learning enterprises are based on some form of partnership. We have already mentioned two, one in the higher education sector in Canada; the other a further education collaboration in the UK. But such joint ventures are by no means the exclusive domain of colleges and universities. There are many cases of e-learning development partnerships in the corporate sector and between business and academe. Anglia Water's University of Water runs honours degrees in partnerships with universities. One of these is an MSc awarded by the University of Buckingham that the company shares with Virgin, Sainsbury's and other companies. Lloyds TSB reports 'improved partnerships with academic and other external institutions in the development of learning activities' (DTI 2000). In the partnership between the University of British Columbia (UBC) and the Monterrey Institute of Technology (ITESM), Mexico, ITESM plays a key role in handling the enrolment and assessment of the Latin American students (see p. 41).

The benefits of partnerships are:

- wider market opportunities
- shared risk
- access to specialist skills
- access to accreditation
- shared know-how.

LEARNING OUTCOMES

E-learning offers a range of benefits, including easier access to learning opportunities and greater learner participation.

Improvements in skills

The e-learning participant not only acquires skills in the subject-matter that is the focus of their study but also improves their performance in secondary or enabling skills such as IT, time management and writing (sometimes known as 'key' or 'transferable' skills).

Greater participation

Well-designed e-learning programmes require all learners to participate by answering questions and undertaking activities that entail communicating not only with a tutor but also with other learners. Learners receive greater equality of treatment, partly due to the lack of the visual cues that influence the class teacher.

Access to resources

Studying an e-learning package can bring learners into contact with a variety of resources and media. In the case of online learning, exposure to the Web offers access to a limitless range of resources and access is available at any time.

Increase in people seeking accreditation

Corporate e-learning managers report significantly increased numbers of individuals taking some form of accredited learning. E-learning systems linked to learning management systems help both organization and individual employees to achieve their objectives (see Chapter 12).

Description of the programme

The product description should include the following:

- title
- scope
- duration (in learner hours)
- outcomes
- summary content
- study method
- media
- learner prerequisites
- accreditation/associated qualifications
- price
- support
- availability

You will need to describe any ancillary materials, for example those for tutors, mentors, trainees or assessors.

If you are preparing the product for sale you will also need:

- a description of the physical components to be sold
- the target markets (for example individuals, organizations, service providers)
- data collected from potential purchasers about their requirements
- a list of competing products with their strengths and weaknesses
- the benefits of the proposed product over its competitors.

This kind of market and competitor analysis will form an important part of your business case.

Figure 3.3 is the description of the entry level numeracy programme developed by the University for Industry for delivery in Learndirect centres; Figure 3.4 gives details of one of the courses within the programme.

Entry level numeracy	Entry levels 1, 2, 3
Target audience	New learners to numeracy
Learner outcomes	To give learners increased confidence in their ability to handle number problems To enable learners to deal with problems involving number at QCA Entry Levels 1, 2, 3 To enable learners to progress to a Level 1 course in numeracy or other preferred options at that level To enable learners to gather sufficient evidence for accreditation at entry level in numeracy To prepare learners for the appropriate written test for entry level numeracy
Qualifications/level	Numeracy entry levels 1, 2, 3

Figure 3.3   Specification for the UfI numeracy skills suite

Financial forecast

Any business plan will need to set out costs and benefits. More specifically, some will need to estimate the income to be derived from the sale of the programme – some, but not all, programmes will be developed for internal use. In these cases whilst no income will be generated it may still be necessary to quantify (in financial terms) the expected benefits.

The e-learning champion will usually be expected to demonstrate a pay-off. For the e-learning innovator at the Forensic Science Service the pay-off was cost-effectiveness: 'I had to show that on-line training was cheaper than external classroom training' (Hiscock, 2000).

Course:	Numbers direct – Addition Stage 1
Description:	Addition Stage 1 is one of a series of programmes covering numbers, money, time measure and shape and data handling, which are aimed at learners who have not had the opportunity to acquire or develop basic numeracy skills. This colourful presentation introduces additions with totals up to 10. It concentrates on the practical use of numbers in day-to-day activities and requires few literacy skills.
Study method:	Offline (CD-ROM or print)
Qualification level:	Awaiting details
Prerequisites:	None
Estimated duration:	4 hours
Price:	Contact a Learndirect centre

Figure 3.4   Details of one of Ufl's basic skills courses

COSTS

You can analyse costs under three categories, as in Figure 3.5.

Cost type	Description
Capital and recurrent costs	Capital costs include the purchase of equipment or materials Recurrent costs occur on an on-going basis (for example computer support)
Production and delivery costs	Production costs are incurred in developing a programme Delivery costs are the costs of 'teaching' the programme
Fixed costs and variable costs	Fixed costs are unaffected by student numbers (for example course design); variable costs are affected (for example tutoring)

Figure 3.5   Analysing costs

Many factors will affect the start-up costs for a new e-learning project. Questions affecting costs include:

- Will materials be purpose-developed or bought off-the-shelf?
- Will purpose-developed materials be commissioned or produced in-house?
- What delivery methods will be used?
- Is the existing provision of computers adequate to support learning?
- Will new premises be required (for example a learning centre)?
- Will new staff be needed?
- What level of on-going tutor support will be required?
- How will the scheme be promoted?
- Will training be available to all or to particular groups?

These factors will vary in significance depending on the scope of the e-learning programme. Within the same university one enthusiastic lecturer may develop a scheme for a single module taken by the students within a particular cohort while in another department a well-funded team may produce an entire graduate programme.

Similar differences apply in the corporate context. At one end of the scale is the case of a small enterprise buying an off-the-shelf package on spreadsheet accounting for their book-keeper to run on an existing PC. They will incur a negligible cost for the materials – possibly less than £100. At the other extreme, a large business corporation intending to convert a significant element of its training programme to an e-learning format will have a very different scale of decision to take. The upfront costs of setting up an in-house development team will be substantial and will need to be evaluated against commissioning external suppliers. We discuss this issue in more detail in Chapter 11.

Many large business applications of e-learning depend on acquiring and distributing off-the-shelf materials. A large corporation or government department will often need to provide a wide variety of training on a repetitive basis in topics such as IT, health and safety, management skills, communications, finance and customer care. (Over half of US companies that use online training teach programming and application software skills.) The total demand could extend to dozens of courses. In such cases, if there are relevant commercially available materials, the purchase cost will compare favourably with developing original materials because 'creating high quality interactive Web content is expensive'.

The key question you need to be able to answer in evaluating these options is 'How many learners will be taking each course?' Research conducted by an American journal revealed that one vendor of commercially produced courses dropped its rates by 50 per cent for a 500-user, one-year, licence if more than 100 titles were purchased. In the USA the numbers can get quite large. In 1999 CBT systems won a $5.7 million contract to deliver 500 courses to Compaq's 30 000 staff. This type of training strategy is quite alien to the average college or university where off-the-shelf materials are far less commonly used.

It may be necessary to develop new materials, for example where no materials exist or where existing products are unsatisfactory. We cover this option in later chapters.

Costs of materials are the most immediate and visible cost. But you also need to consider the costs of delivery (including tutor support) and of marketing the programme.

When the decisions have been made about sourcing materials, delivery systems and marketing strategy the project manager can begin to assess all the various costs involved. Figure 3.6 shows the categories of cost that might need to be taken into account.

E-learning cost	Categories
Human resources – salaries	Subject expert Internet specialist Developer Tutor Graphic artist Administrator
Human resources – training	Designer training Tutor training Administrator training
Equipment	Server PCs Video-conferencing Learning centre furnishing
Support	Library Resource centre Help line
Materials	Off-the-shelf packages Printed support materials Copyright licenses
Marketing	Printing Exhibitions

Figure 3.6 Categories of cost

Case study: Fixed costs and variable costs

We shall look at the fixed and variable costs method in the context of a case study – a programme on the Design and Delivery of Technology Based Distributed Learning developed by the University of British Columbia (UBC) in partnership with the Monterrey Institute of Technology, Mexico (ITESM). This was the first of five programmes developed towards a postgraduate certificate in technology-based distributed learning. The data are extracted from *Investing in Online Learning: Potential Benefits and Limitations* by Sylvia Bartolic-Zlomislic and Tony Bates of the University of British Columbia and reproduced with their kind permission.

Table 3.1 shows the costs involved in developing the UBC/ITESM e-learning programme. Notice the significant percentage allocated to tutoring. Besides the internal tutors the programme required the participation of several external experts in the field.

The aggregate total for the first year is remarkably close to a figure cited for New York University. Gerald A. Heeger, Dean of the School of Continuing and Professional Studies at NYU was quoted as saying that 'putting a course on-line and supporting it costs about $50,000' (*Arenson*, 1998).

Table 3.1   Costs of an e-learning programme

Cost source	1997 $	1998 $	1999 $	2000 $	Total $
Fixed costs:					
Subject experts	12 000	4 000	4 000	4 000	24 000
Internet specialist	2 100	1 500	1 500	1 500	6 600
Design	1 200	300			1 500
New procedures	6 000				6 000
Marketing	3 000	3 000	3 000	3 000	12 000
Server	300				300
Departmental overheads	6 150	2 200	2 125	2 125	12 600
Library	1 000				1 000
Copyright clearance	700	700	700	700	2 800
International tutors	3 000	3 000	3 000	3 000	12 000
Total fixed costs	35 450	14 700	14 325	14 325	78 800
Variable costs					
Tutoring (department)	8 800	8 200	8 200	7 040	32 240
Tutoring (others)		5 000	5 000		10 000
Delivery	3 021	4 822	4 822	2 572	15 237
Faculty: 5% of gross	2 014	2 247	2 247	1 320	7 828
Total variable costs	13 835	20 269	20 269	10 932	65 305
Total costs	49 285	34 969	34 594	25 257	144 105

Revenues

In some cases the e-learning manager will not be concerned with income. A case in point is a programme director at a university who redesigns for Web delivery a course module that was previously taught in the classroom. The overall course fee charged to students may well be unaffected. The development costs may be met by a source of special funding or from an in-house source, for example an innovation fund. In the corporate sector, the manager may be given a budget to develop learning opportunities for employees for whom the programme may be free of charge.

Often the manager will be required to identify ways in which the programme can generate additional income. The UBC/ITESM course is just such an example. Over the life of the first course and the complete programme of five courses, all course development and delivery costs were expected to be fully recoverable from fees. Table 3.2 shows a breakdown of projected revenues for the UBC programme.

New York University adopted a similar approach. Its online programme is financed by a for-profit subsidiary with a view to developing and selling specialized online courses primarily to other institutions but also to individuals.

The business plan should also attempt to quantify the wider benefits of e-learning, those going beyond the direct generation of income. Hence you should seek to quantify such benefits as increased access to the development of new skills and savings on travel and time away from the workplace.

Table 3.2   The UBC/ITESM Educational Studies course: projected revenue

	1997 $	1998 $	1999 $	2000 $	Total $
Student numbers					
Graduate	11	12	12	8	
Certificate	29	48	48	24	
Source of revenue					
UBC graduate fees @ 464/student	5 115	5 580	5 580	3 720	19 995
Certificate fees @ 695/student	20 155	33 360	33 360	16 680	103 555
ITESM (Monterrey) rights payment	15 000	6 000	6 000	6 000	33 000
Total revenue	40 270	44 940	44 940	26 400	156 550

The marketing plan

The Chartered Institute of Marketing defines marketing as 'the management process which identifies, anticipates and supplies customer requirements efficiently and profitably'. This usefully reminds us that marketing is more than just promotion. The marketing plan should include evidence of need and of how the proposed programme meets this need (see Chapter 4 for more on the stages of market identification and analysis that should precede programme development).

The Small Firms Enterprise Development Initiative points out that 'You need to understand your market to sell your products and services at a profit. The detail of what you need to look at will depend on your type of business and the sort of customers you will be selling to.' (SFEDI 2000).

In the e-learning market, business and customer types vary greatly. There are at least three quite different types of business or institution who will need to prepare a marketing plan for e-learning. These are illustrated in the following scenarios which have been selected to illustrate the variety of applications that makes generalization so difficult.

Scenario 1: The e-learning manager in a company is setting up a scheme to provide job training and general skills training (for example IT, written communications) to staff in several locations.

Scenario 2: The course leader of a post-graduate diploma course in a university is converting the course from evening class delivery to e-learning.

Scenario 3: A small e-learning consultancy has produced an off-the-shelf package on quality for organizations aiming to achieve ISO9000 accreditation.

These differences in circumstance make it difficult, if not impossible, to produce a single checklist or set of guidelines valid for any e-learning marketing plan. We hope that whatever your context you will be able to take from the guidelines that follow those that are relevant to you.

HOW THE MARKETING PLAN RELATES TO THE BUSINESS PLAN

The marketing plan may be a separate document or a separate section within the business plan. Many of the features of the business plan that we have already reviewed relate to marketing, including the description of the end users (see Chapter 1), the course costs and revenues, and the expected benefits.

A marketing plan should begin with clear objectives. There is likely to be a strong link back to the business plan here. For example one of the key features of the business plan for the UBC/ITESM e-learning scheme was to attract enrolment from Latin American students via the ITESM connection. The marketing plan will need to show how these end users are to be identified and what promotional strategies will be employed to target them. This is a variation on our Scenario 2 example. In a Scenario 1 context the business plan for a multinational launching e-learning to its staff in, say, 40 countries would probably show a significant return on investment compared with the class taught programmes or *ad hoc* locally supplied distance learning materials that were previously used. The objectives of the marketing strategy for the new e-learning system will need to reflect the special requirements of this internal market. For instance it may have to address issues such as the attitudes of local line managers and trainers as well as those of the employees who are the end users.

The costs in the e-learning business plan spreadsheet are likely to include an aggregate figure for marketing. The marketing plan should demonstrate how this figure is made up under headings such as graphic design, surveys and interviews with potential customers, discounts to vendors, mail costs, printing, TV/radio advertisements, website design, exhibition stand hire and enquiries. These headings may be grouped under fixed costs (for example printing) and variable costs (for example answering enquiries).

DESCRIBING THE PRODUCT FEATURES AND BENEFITS

We have seen how the business plan may include a general description of the product and of the expected benefits of the e-learning strategy. The marketing plan can restate these general benefits but should be more specific about the particular content and benefits of the product.

Programme designers may feel that the benefits will be obvious from a brief glance at the product description. However, it will be important to spell them out because, as we shall see, many parties may be involved in the decision to buy, and later in creating the circumstances in which successful learning takes place. Furthermore, the different groups will be looking for different benefits, for example while learners might be seeking a package that is enjoyable to use, line managers will be more interested in a reduction in staff time spent away from work. Make a point of highlighting any of these benefits that you can claim for your programme:

Pay-off: Passing this course improves chances of gaining a qualification.
There is a link to personal advancement.
Achievement scores are higher by this method.
Learners are more likely to achieve a standard score.

Added value: Learners in distance locations can interact with each other.

There is less work for managers/tutors.

Diagnostic testing and a modular format enables learning in planned stages.

Users become more confident in using computers.

Convenience: This way is faster than other methods.

There is less travel.

Learning can take place at home/the desktop/the company learning centre.

Learning can take place at any time.

PILOTING

In Chapter 2 we strongly recommended that you pilot your programme at the development stage. This also offers a marketing opportunity: you can choose potential users/purchasers as pilot sites. One of the authors developed packages on mentoring and coaching and piloted these in government departments, major companies and small businesses. Some of these pilot sites subsequently purchased the finished product and continued to use it over a number of years.

When planning the pilot you need to consider how many learners to involve and how much of the programme to trial; you also need to consider the costs and how these will be met.

KNOWING YOUR MARKET

If we consider the three scenarios (company trainer, university tutor and commercial vendor) it will become apparent that the 'market' in the sense of the purchasers of e-learning can be rather more complex than may first appear. There are sometimes principal and secondary markets and there are also actors to take into account who influence purchasing decisions, for example see Figure 3.7. Each group has a different priority; each will need a distinctive marketing message related to their needs, as illustrated in Figure 3.8

Group	Contribution
Senior managers	Give general endorsement
Budget-holders	Pay for the programme
Line managers	Release employees
Trainers	Help learners complete the programme
Learners	Join the programme

Figure 3.7   Market analysis

Group	Message
Senior managers	Leading edge, use of latest technology
Budget-holders	Most cost-effective way to deliver the required learning
Line managers	Programme is flexible in time and place, and delivers results
Trainers	You can develop new skills, your role is key to learners' success
Learners	You'll enjoy taking this programme and you will find it useful

Figure 3.8   Tailoring the message to the market

The marketing plan should include details of how the necessary messages will reach the various players (sometimes summarized as 'promotional methods'). These may be face-to-face (such as events or visits by salespeople) or mediated (such as a newsletters or e-mails). Marketing also overlaps with learner support (see Chapter 8): activities such as responding to enquirers could be defined as mainly 'marketing' or mainly 'learner support'. The important point is that such activities are not forgotten.

CASE STUDY: AUTOMEDON

Consider the case of a Scenario 3 company – an e-learning consultancy called Automedon. The MD of Automedon in visiting a number of large financial institutions has discovered that business letter writing is one of the most commonly delivered courses during induction training in such companies. As a result Automedon produces a four-hour learning package entitled *Successful Business Letters* designed to replace or support the existing classroom training. The package is available on CD-ROM or in a Web-delivered version. Besides selling the package direct Automedon also makes a last minute deal to sell through specialist vendors

The fictional case of Automedon describes a modest venture in the selling of one package. Other new e-learning ventures will be more ambitious. However, it is probably not a good idea to extend your inventory of titles too rapidly. New York University may be a model worth emulating. It started by offering a narrower range of programmes that had a broad demand, such as IT, management, real estate and credit analysis. As Gerald A. Heeger commented: 'The issue here is not to have thousands of courses but to have highly focused courses that meet large needs' (Arenson, 1998).

The business plan also needs to address how the product will reach customers and how any payments will be managed. The adoption of an e-learning strategy can cause problems with traditional payment practices in institutions. At UBC the bookshop previously had no special arrangements for international distance learning students. The shop insisted on payment before despatching materials. Delays in processing international money orders caused students corresponding delays in meeting their study schedules. The solution was to develop a one-stop shopping strategy. The e-learning office took over the tasks of ordering the materials from the bookshop and despatching them to students when ordered.

AN ACTION PLAN

Finally, the marketing plan will need to set out what has to be done, when, by whom and with what resource. Figure 3.9 shows a simple list of activities, some of which can be carried out in parallel. Given the considerable variability between programmes, the second and third columns are left for you to complete; you may need to delete some items and add new activities relevant to your own context.

Month	Activity	Person responsible	Resource
	Draw up programme specification Decide sale price/fees Set up payment methods Design printed and electronic promotional materials Draw up mailing list for leaflets Prepare public media advertising Identify internet-based networks (that is people who share an interest in the subject and who can promote the package) Design programme website Despatch leaflets (phase 1) Devise demos and place on website Use internal e-mail to promote the scheme Establish accreditation status Design in-house certification (external accreditation unavailable) Devise enrolment procedure Prepare support materials package Identify vendor agencies Compile pilot test data Send out phase 2 leaflets Run presentations to managers and potential students Write journal articles and book/s Enter the scheme for awards Identify and attend conferences (to speak) and exhibitions (to exhibit)		

Figure 3.9   The marketing plan: activity scheduling

SUMMARY

· ·

In this chapter we have seen how the complex business of setting up and implementing an e-learning programme can be facilitated by making a business plan and a marketing plan. Depending on the circumstances these may be separate documents or two parts of the same document.

The business/marketing plan should:

- demonstrate the value of the scheme
- reflect the organization's corporate goals
- clarify the benefits accruing from the use of the technology
- include a financial forecast (and demonstrate the return on investment if appropriate)
- include a detailed specification of the programme
- demonstrate an understanding of the market and the needs of different customer types
- demonstrate added value (for example how the scheme attracts new types of learner)
- clarify means of access and payment.

In addition, if appropriate, it should:

- include ancillary production and delivery plans
- explain the accreditation process.

4 *Analysing Learning Needs*

THIS CHAPTER WILL HELP YOU:

- place needs analysis within the wider design process
- use an analytical approach to improving performance within an organization
- identify examples of where learning will improve performance
- distinguish 'reactive' and 'proactive' approaches to performance analysis
- carry out goal analysis to identify learning needs
- survey particular learner groups to identify learning needs.

An overview of the training design process

We know that somebody has learned when they can do something that they were previously incapable of doing. Another way of putting this is to say that learning is verified through performance. Good learning programmes lead the learner to demonstrate the skills and understanding they previously lacked.

We can all remember attending classes that seemed a waste of time. Either we already knew a lot about the topic or it was irrelevant to our needs. Thus before setting out on the challenging and expensive business of developing an e-learning programme we must be sure that it will meet a genuine need and that it is the way to meet that need. At the other end – when the learners complete the programme – we need to assess how well they have learned. As Figure 4.1 indicates, these two requirements – verifying needs and assessing achievement – are two of the four stages of the training design process at the macro level.

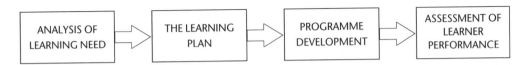

Figure 4.1 The stages of learning design

NEEDS ANALYSIS

Training is expensive and readily attracts the attention of management. Staff away on courses, the print department producing manuals, the computer being used to score tests: these and other activities signal to management that training means spending. Hence learning needs analysis: to ensure that the expense of training can be justified.

Over the past 30 years it has become commonplace to hear expert speakers at training conferences stress the need to conduct a thorough needs analysis before a package is designed and produced. Even so it seems to be one of the hardest lessons for companies to learn. Here is a typical, and true, example.

CASE STUDY: BUILDINGS INSURANCE

A financial institution sells two similar buildings insurance products. Product A – for borrowers who have existing mortgages with the company – sells very well. However sales of Product B – for customers who have mortgages with other lenders – are running well below target. The training department is commissioned by the Insurance Department to develop a programme on Product B because, says the Insurance Department, 'Branch staff don't understand the features and benefits of the product.' Visits to one or two branches by a training designer reveal that the staff are equally well acquainted with both products. However, selling Product A generates credits for the staff that convert into salary bonuses. Selling Product B gains no credits. Although the problem clearly cannot be solved by training, the Insurance Department insists and the programme is developed anyway.

So the moral must be think before you train. Examples of situations in which this type of needs analysis could have been profitably employed are cited regularly in the news media. The terrible fire that occurred at London's King's Cross Station in November 1987 was followed by a public enquiry. *The Independent* reported:

> A fire hydrant only 50 yards from the escalator at the heart of the King's Cross fire was not used because an underground official did not recognise it.
> Philip Brickell, a ticket collector, stood a few feet away from the hydrant but did not spot it because he 'had forgotten what they looked like' . . .
> A fire extinguisher at the foot of the escalator was also overlooked. Mr Brickell was worried it would have interfered with electrical equipment.

Training is an obvious solution to this problem but it is not the only nor necessarily the best solution. Might not redesigning the hydrants and locating them so that they were unmistakable be more effective? It is, in fact, what was done.

In this chapter we describe three approaches to learning needs analysis:

- performance analysis
- goal analysis, which turns statements of general need into specific statements of behaviour
- people-focused analysis, which involves a survey of the people within an organization, profiling the capabilities of staff (associated with appraisal schemes and the UK Investors in People initiative).

You can use each on its own, or in combination with the others.

Performance analysis

Organizations naturally wish to maximize their performance. To do this they embark (more or less systematically) on performance analysis, particularly to:

- diagnose problems and how to overcome them
- raise satisfactory performance to a higher level.

Indicators of a problem could include:

- increased customer complaints
- above average levels of staff absence
- higher than usual wastage
- accidents.

A performance analysis aims to pinpoint the causes of ineffective performance.

Figure 4.2 shows two main routes to performance improvement: one through people factors and one through other factors. These are further sub-divided; note that the examples shown are only indicative – other factors could be added.

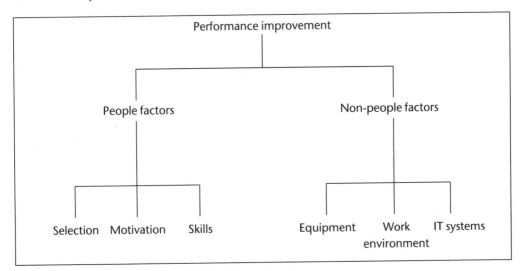

Figure 4.2   Performance improvement factors

The distinction between people and non-people factors is crude but it does show that a performance problem can have several causes. In particular, for our purposes here, the way to improve performance will not necessarily be improving peoples' skills through learning. It may be more appropriate to bring in better equipment or to improve the environment in which employees are working.

One of the early exponents of this type of analysis, Joe Harless, described three causes of sub-standard performance, as shown in Figure 4.3 (Harless 1975). The first two reasons for deficient performance have non-training solutions: improving the working environment and improving motivation. Remedies to non-training problems include:

People fail to perform correctly because	Example	Solution
They are hindered by their working conditions	Filing system badly designed	Redesign job or environment
They don't want to do it (they lack motivation)	Working faster means longer queues	Provide better incentives, improve the quality of feedback to staff
They don't know how (they lack skills and knowledge)	Can't use new browser	Training

Figure 4.3   Analysing deficient performance

- providing job aids such as cue cards and ready reckoners
- redesigning the job
- redesigning systems (for example filing)
- redesigning documentation
- providing a regular system of feedback on achievement.

The third example in the table *is* addressable by providing learning opportunities, though even here we should note the possibility of other solutions, such as recruiting new staff with the required skills and knowledge.

We have been using the terms performance 'problem' and 'deficient' performance but a similar analysis can be used to improve performance that is already adequate, to make it even better. Many organizations these days aspire not just to competence but to excellence. Learning at all levels in the organization is key to this.

REACTIVE AND PROACTIVE PERFORMANCE ANALYSIS

Performance analysis can be reactive or proactive. In the former case, existing performance is the subject of analysis. Proactive analysis is used when an organization has to anticipate or prepare for a future challenge such as the introduction of new systems or procedures. In these circumstances it may well be that few, if any, existing staff possess relevant knowledge or skills.

The two modes of performance analysis are illustrated in Figure 4.4. Example R1 illustrates reactive performance analysis of a general or company-wide problem; R2 is a training needs analysis for a specific work group. Of the two examples of proactive performance analysis P1 takes place at the general level; P2 concerns one person only.

Modes		
	Reactive	**Proactive**
General	R1 *New logistics system installed six months ago but not used fully* ALL HEAD OFFICE STAFF ABOVE GRADE 2 NEED TRAINING	P1 *We're implementing a new staff appraisal system* ALL STAFF WILL NEED SOME TRAINING
Job Specific	R2 *Customers complain of waiting time for simple repairs* TRAIN SALESPEOPLE IN BASIC MAINTENANCE	P2 *We're getting a bookkeeping package* TRAIN SECRETARY IN SAGE

Figure 4.4   Modes of performance analysis

(Note that the problem is stated in italics; the hypothetical training solution is in upper case.)

CASE STUDY: DECIMALIZATION

Consider for example the introduction of decimalization in the UK in 1971. To implement this required a wide variety of skills such as change-giving, writing invoices, calculating and verbal skills. Conventional, group-based training was quite inadequate to cope with the situation. The employee numbers were too vast and the subject experts too thin on the ground. As a consequence, many companies commissioned self-instructional packages or instructor-support kits, comprising all the necessary lesson plans, exercises and aids for local supervisors to conduct their own training. Modular learning materials meant that employees were able to develop only those skills relevant to their tasks: needs analysis helps ensure training is focused.

In an e-learning context it is becoming increasingly common to bring together a number of different approaches to performance improvement. Learning materials and performance aids can be combined within a single system known as an electronic performance support system (EPSS). An EPSS usually includes a variety of features including computer-based training units, examples of the outputs of tasks, reference materials and so forth. The screen shown in Figure 4.5 is an example of an EPSS designed to help companies get started in the Investors in People system.

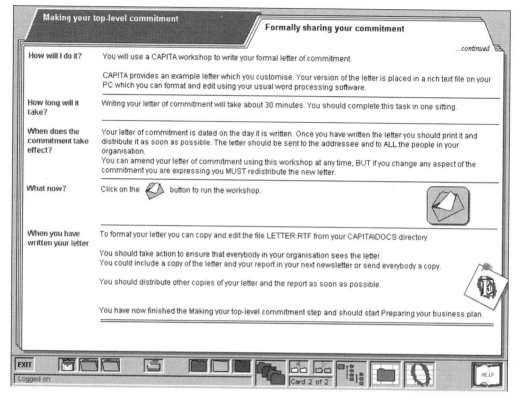

Figure 4.5   EPSS screen

CASE STUDY: CAPITA

The CAPITA package was produced by Dean Interactive Learning Limited. CAPITA was designed to help organizations wishing to become Investors in People (IIP) to implement and maintain the necessary systems and procedures. The features of CAPITA are:

- a planning system that comprises a step-by-step guide through the whole IIP process
- guidance tools (for exampled action planners, templates and examples of documents)

- information about the national standard
- individual training and development portfolios
- a glossary.

The screen shown in Figure 4.5 assists in the development of the formal letter of commitment. The user can choose to receive guidance in the 'workshop' (accessible through the envelope button), see an example (through the E button) or format the letter using a template.

Goal analysis

Goal analysis (first described by R. F. Mager) often takes place as a natural consequence of a performance analysis. Where a skill/knowledge improvement is deemed necessary it may be initially expressed in rather vague terminology. For example the manager of a car showroom deduces from the volume of customer complaints that the general level of telephone answering needs improving. He tells the training officer that staff need 'to get better at answering the phone'. Goal analysis is a methodology for converting such aspirations and good intentions into the precise descriptions of the desired performance.

The stages of goal analysis are shown in Figure 4.6. Each step takes us away from vague aspirations towards clear statements of identifiable behaviour.

Step	ACTION	COMMENTS
1	Write down the goal	Describe *outcomes* not process. An example of an outcome for the car dealer case would be 'Calls will be answered quickly and in a friendly and polite manner.'
2	Jot down the actions or words that represent the goal	This is a brainstorming process. Some typical items from this process for the telephone answering goal might be: • be friendly • answer the phone quickly • no interruptions • don't be rude • ask questions to clarify the problem.
3	Analyse the list at Step 2 into 'Performance' or 'Non-performance'	Eliminate duplications, irrelevancies and fuzzies. In our example we would eliminate 'be friendly' and 'don't be rude' because they are both fuzzy and both say the same thing; 'quickly' needs to be made more specific.
4	Write coherent descriptions of the desired performance	There must be acceptable evidence that the goal has been achieved. After eliminating the redundant items this is how we would write the two remaining: • answer within three rings • don't interrupt the caller • ask questions to clarify the problem.
5	Test statements for adequacy	If the learner can do it have they achieved the goal? Is anything missing?

Figure 4.6   The stages of goal analysis

Figure 4.7 illustrates a goal analysis done within a financial institution. The initial aim was 'to know the features and benefits of a product called Megacon'. On the left are the outcomes of Step 2, on the right the outcomes of Step 4. We look further at defining learning outcomes in the next chapter.

To know the product features of Megacon	To be able to sell Megacon
• customers' eligibility • handle objections • claims procedure • what is the premium • know benefits and features • match benefits to needs • complete forms • know needs • opportunity spotting • what time factors are involved • effect of claims	• decide customers' eligibility • calculate premium • list features • identify customer needs • recognize sales opportunity • explain appropriate benefits • respond to objections • select appropriate forms • seek a commitment.
Outcomes of Step 2	**Outcomes of Step 4**

Figure 4.7   A goal analysis on a financial product

People-focused analysis

As we have seen, performance analysis typically starts with a wish to improve individual or group performance. Another starting point to learning needs analysis is to survey the people within the organization – usually all levels of staff are involved. In some organizations it is already possible to link data from personnel records to a learning management system, thus greatly reducing the tedium and time involved in the statistical analysis and the subsequent planning of personal learning experiences. In 1999 the document company Xerox as part of their new learning initiative 'commissioned a bespoke learning management system that links an on-line directory to competency assessments and on-line booking over the coming year' (DTI 2000).

In the past a wide-ranging macro survey of all staff would only take place in exceptional circumstances, for example where a new general manager felt that an ailing organization was generally lacking in technical, managerial or operational competence or where new and generally unfamiliar systems were replacing conventional methods. In the UK the introduction of national vocational qualifications (NVQs) stimulated large-scale, continuous needs analysis. The Investors in People strategy prompted companies to assess their personnel against relevant NVQ frameworks to devise personal learning plans. The rapidly growing interest in learning management systems has led to growth in needs analysis as a continuous process (see also Chapter 12) .

Organizations can obtain information about training needs at the macro level in three ways.

1 *The group level.* A group is surveyed, together with their supervisors, internal customers and their subordinates. The focus is on group responses and usually leads to group development events. Each person ticks items on a large inventory of statements (for example *Common tasks and problems are not tackled together, We don't make the best use of resources*). Computer analysis of the results produces a list of problem areas within the organization (for example teamwork, use of resources), in rank order.

2 *The organizational audit.* An audit is held to review production, financial, personnel and operational data from records and reports. Data might include staff turnover rates, rejects on the production line and job inventories. Here the focus is on 'results' of activities and you then work backwards from this to the causes to identify learning needs.

3 *The individual level.* The achievement levels, knowledge, behaviour, and skills of individual members of staff are explored; the focus is on the developmental needs of individuals and the outcome may include individual development plans. This is the approach of the Investors in People programme. Questionnaires are widely used. They often require the job performer to rate tasks that they perform, using criteria such as importance and frequency.

A variety of survey techniques may be used. Figure 4.8 shows those which are the most suitable for each of the approaches. Figure 4.9 is an extract taken from a simple checklist for supervisors.

Approach	Survey techniques
1 Group survey	Learning needs survey, employee attitude survey, consumer survey, interviews
2 Organizational audit	Production records, personnel records, functional audits, skills inventory
3 Individual needs	Interviews, learning needs questionnaire, performance appraisal data, observation

Figure 4.8   Survey techniques for learning needs analysis

Please read the list carefully before answering. Circle 'Yes' if you believe you need training in that skill, either for use in your current job or for promotion to a better position. Circle '?' if you are uncertain. Circle 'No' if you feel that you have no need for training in that area.

1 How to supervise minority workers	Yes	?	No
2 How to train staff efficiently	Yes	?	No
3 How to handle discipline problems	Yes	?	No
4 How to conform to safety requirements in my department	Yes	?	No
5 How to develop better objectives with my staff	Yes	?	No
6 How to improve my personal productivity	Yes	?	No
7 How to implement participative management	Yes	?	No
	Yes	?	No

Figure 4.9   Learning needs checklist (individual)

The type of large-scale needs analysis that IIP and other people-focused approaches entails requires a major commitment from both management and staff. All concerned must make a significant effort to maintain the system. At times it may appear that a lot of people are spending a lot of time on it for little return. However, when one considers that a process of continuous analysis could well have avoided some of the major disasters of the past 20 years (such as the King's Cross fire, the *Herald of Free Enterprise* sinking or the Paddington rail crash – in all of which lack of training was a significant factor), the effort may well be considered worthwhile.

SUMMARY

- Needs analysis may take place in a number of modes.
- Performance problem solving may be proactive or reactive; it may involve a single individual or a group.
- A performance problem analysis may suggest other solutions to performance problems than training.
- Goal analysis aims to clarify vague or general aspirations by redefining them in measurable terms.
- People-focused needs analysis is a continuous process often involving an entire organization; it entails collecting and reviewing data gathered from interviews, questionnaires, and so on.

5 Defining and Testing Learning Outcomes

THIS CHAPTER WILL HELP YOU:

- describe the benefits of specifying learning outcomes
- identify well-defined learning outcomes
- write effective learning outcomes
- identify what learners will already know/be able to do before they join the programme
- design assessment tests for learning outcomes.

The previous chapter looked at different ways of identifying learning needs. The next step is to turn these into outcomes. Key questions to be asked are:

- What do learners need to be able to do?
- How will I recognize that learning has taken place?
- What do the learners know already?

When you specify the outcomes you will also be thinking about assessment: how you will check whether learners achieve the outcomes. You will need to consider the activities in which learners will need to engage both to learn and to show the outcome of their learning.

Figure 5.1 (which you first met in Chapter 1 (p. 6) shows the place of these processes within the development of a programme.

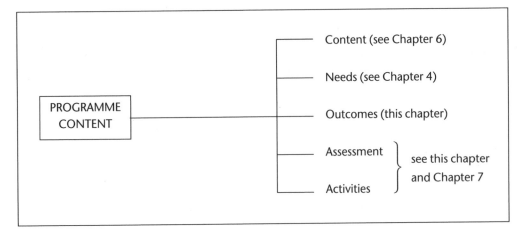

Figure 5.1   Programme development

Learning outcomes and their benefits

Learning outcomes (sometimes called 'objectives') help the learner to understand the new capabilities they are seeking to acquire. Outcomes can be phrased in varying levels of detail. A programme for new bank staff could include a 40-minute unit on checking paying-in slips. The learning outcome would be very specific, for example:

> *Given 15 payslips from different customers identify those that are incorrectly completed and circle the error/s in each case.*

On the other hand, the learning outcome for an entire programme would be much wider in scope. Here is the learning outcome for a programme on customer care comprising eight modules run over two days:

> *Participants will achieve consistently high standards of customer satisfaction in the areas of identifying customer needs, communications, handling complaints and providing added value.*

Figure 5.2 shows the various levels at which outcomes can be set, ranging from general capabilities to very specific skills and applications. Outcomes at the most general level are often set by management. Programme developers have to translate these into specific statements of learner performance.

Level of outcome	Example (from the insurance industry)
Continuing outcomes	Keep updated on new insurance products and modifications to existing policies and become more proactive in exploiting selling opportunities
End of programme outcomes	Be able to describe the key features of all the company's insurance products, matching each product to suitable customers
Module outcomes	Given customer enquiries about the Safecon policy: • identify those for whom the product is most likely to be suitable. • help a customer to complete all the necessary documentation for a Safecon proposal
Specific performance outcomes (linked to a section or unit within a module)	Given descriptions of six applicants for Safecon, identify any who are ineligible Calculate the Safecon premium for each of the following customers

Figure 5.2   Example of different levels of outcomes (selling insurance)

In this chapter we concentrate on outcomes at the more specific end of the scale. The following examples are drawn from three very different areas: nursing, computer logic and bridge.

EXAMPLES

From a course on lifting and carrying for nurses
At the end of this session learners will be able to:

- identify on diagrams the key points of posture required for lifting with reference to the feet, back legs, head, arms and hands
- given illustrations of good and bad lifts, identify the correct method of lifting
- on a diagram of the body label the muscles that should be used in lifting
- score at least 10 marks out of a possible 12 in a final test.

From a text on computer logic
On completion of this programme learners will be able to:

- convert whole numbers and fractions between the binary, octal and decimal numbering systems
- obtain 100 per cent on a test comprising nine problems

From a programme on bridge
This programme will help you learn how to:

- evaluate a selection of hands according to point-count and honour-trick systems
- as dealer, select an opening bid for a selection of hands of 11 to 15 points, no hand having more than one five-card suit.

ACHIEVING INTERACTION

E-learning programmes should be interactive. This distinguishes them from textbooks, videos and other one-way media for transmitting information. The designer of the package achieves interaction by asking questions and posing problems. The learner responds to the problems and receives feedback on their response. Figure 5.3 demonstrates feedback to learners in an e-learning programme.

But the questions have to be relevant and linked to the learning outcomes. A brief inspection of half a dozen packages taken at random suggests that many authors proceed as follows: they begin to write a script and, at a certain point, usually at the end of the page or towards the bottom of the screen because they think that it's about time, they ask a question. At the top of the page when they started writing they had no idea what question they were going to ask. This approach very often results in trivial or irrelevant questions. Technically it may be interaction but it certainly doesn't lead to learning.

The questions and problems on which interaction depends should derive from the learning outcomes. These in turn will derive from the goal analysis (see Chapter 4). Figure 5.4 illustrates the pathway to interaction.

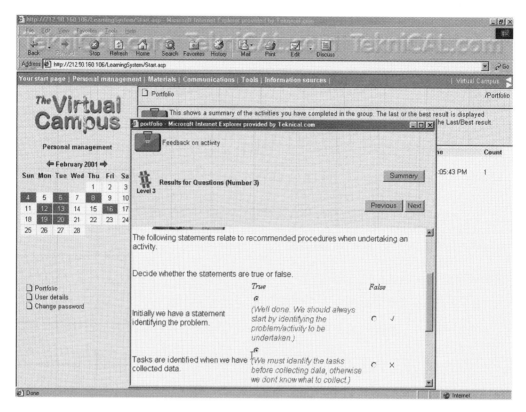

Figure 5.3   Feedback to learners in an online programme

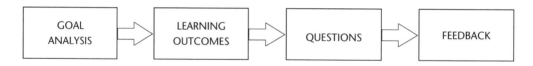

Figure 5.4   The pathway to interaction

WHO BENEFITS FROM LEARNING OUTCOMES

Learning outcomes help the various stakeholders:

- sponsors can assess the value of their investment
- accrediting bodies can measure learner achievement
- learners can monitor their progress
- training designers can plan learning programmes.

How to write effective outcomes

In the three examples shown on p. 61, the skill or behaviour to be acquired is described by a performance type verb: identify, label, convert, evaluate, select. The more specific the performance described in an outcome, the more helpful it will be to the stakeholders. It will also help you in setting assessments of performance. The verb describes the performance to be learned. The other two components are:

- a description of the conditions under which the performance is to be practised
- a statement of the standard or criterion for performance.

The example in Figure 5.5 shows these three components.

Performance	Conditions	Standards
Trainees will be able to state the meaning of road signs on UK roads	Given 15 colour images of signs chosen at random from a complete set	All correct within 20 seconds

Figure 5.5   A fully expressed learning outcome

THE VERB

A well-framed learning outcome communicates the trainer/author's intent. Most people would agree the verb to be the most important feature. Verbs used to define objectives should be positive and describe observable performance wherever possible.

As Figure 5.6 shows, some words do this better than others. Words of the type listed in the right-hand column tell learners more precisely what they may expect from their programme and help designers devise activities relevant to those expectations.

Words open to many interpretations	Words open to fewer interpretations	
to know to understand to appreciate to familiarize to acquaint	to write to label to rank order to identify to compare	to list to choose

Figure 5.6   The verb in a learning outcome

CONDITIONS

The word 'conditions' is used to refer to any special factors that may constrain the performance to be learned. These constraints could be particular clothing that is to be worn for the performance of a task (such as eye protectors), apparatus that may be used (such as a calculator), or the environment in which the performance takes place (for example a busy shop). The condition is often introduced by the word 'given'.

Conditions do not always have to be stated; sometimes they are obvious. But on other occasions to omit the condition might seriously mislead the learner. Take, for example, the outcome

Given a job aid be able to convert gross figures to sums net of VAT.

Without the condition (given on electronic calculators) the learner might try to make the conversion by using the VAT fraction. This would introduce an unnecessary level of difficulty: in this case, manual calculation is not part of the desired outcome. (Note that in this example no standard is specified. Presumably it would be 100 per cent.)

STANDARDS

Performance standards in outcomes may be grouped into four major types: accuracy, completeness, time and safety/security (Figure 5.7).

Accuracy	The most common type, this specifies how well you want your learners to perform and may be expressed as a percentage, as a number (for example, 8 out of 10) or as a measurement, depending on the nature of the task.
Completeness	How much of the task or how many examples learners should undertake to prove their competence. Examples are: • lay sufficient 30 cm floor tiles to cover at least 1 square metre in a corner • given six examples of people applying for mortgage loans, decide which are acceptable.
Time	Should the task be performed within a particular time limit? One would not normally seek to achieve the speed of an experienced performer by the end of a learning programme. However, some tasks by their very nature must be completed within a minimum time limit and this may need to be specified in the learning outcomes. For example certain chemical processes always take place within a particular time frame and the training of process operators must take this into account.
Safety/security	Are there any procedures related to the task that would, if neglected, leave an unsafe or insecure situation? Staff dealing with financial information may perform data entry and calculations perfectly but leaving documents lying around after completing the task would be a sub-standard performance.

Figure 5.7   Types of standard for learning outcomes

Some outcomes may need a combination of these four categories. In the floor laying and mortgage loan examples an accuracy statement would also be desirable, for example:

Given six examples of people applying for mortgage loans, decide which are acceptable with at least five correct decisions)

OUTCOMES SHOULD REFLECT CONTEXT

Learners should perceive outcomes as 'realistic'. Attention to the conditions helps here: as far as possible the outcome should relate to the context in which the learning will be applied. For example an outcome for building society branch managers on deciding loan applications would be more effective if it requires participants to judge real or simulated applications rather than just to 'state the rule for giving advances'.

The way in which outcomes are worded is also important. The examples we have given are versions used by the author for planning purposes. These are precise but rather formal and stilted. When phrasing outcomes for learners a more friendly style will usually be appropriate.

Assessing the outcomes

Once outcomes are clear the designer can move on to consider how these will be assessed. Good outcomes will immediately suggest the kinds of activities that can be used to test achievement. Here is an example:

> **Outcome :** *Given 10 applications for mortgage loans (five from individuals, five from couples), decide which are eligible for a loan and calculate the maximum advance.*
>
> **Test:** *This test comprises six cases. For each case you have to decide if the applicant/s is/are eligible for a loan and calculate the maximum possible advance. Click on the arrow for Case 1.*

As we shall see in Chapter 7, tests can be used at several points: before a learner starts (to identify whether they can already achieve the outcome), during the learning process, or at the end. Figure 5.8 shows the role of tests on entry/pre module and at the end of a module. Before the programme, the entry test asks the questions 'Do learners need the programme? Are they ready for it?' the pre-test asks 'How much do they already know/can they already do?' At the end of the programme the post-test asks 'How much have they learned? Do they need more on this topic?'

ENTRY BEHAVIOUR

In Chapter 1 we stressed the value of listing the characteristics of the participants. As well as personal characteristics, motivations and interests, learners also bring with them a whole range of knowledge and skills more or less relevant to the programme you are designing. This

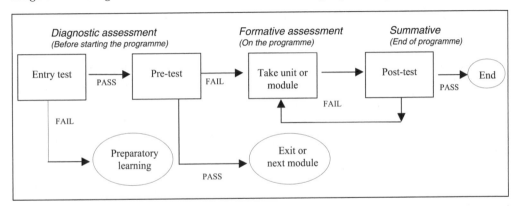

Figure 5.8   Different functions of tests in learning programmes

existing capability is sometimes known as the individual's 'entry behaviour'. A synonymous term introduced as part of the movement towards national standards in the UK is 'prior learning'.

'Programme prerequisites' are the essential capabilities the learner must have in order to commence study. For example learners beginning (or revising) the study of percentages will not be able to progress unless they can perform simple calculations with fractions. Assessment of the learners' existing capabilities may reveal that many individuals have forgotten all they learned at school about fractions. In this case simple calculating with fractions will need to be added to the programme outcomes.

For each skill you determine the learner must have at the end of the programme you must decide whether you will assume that the new learners already have that skill. If 'yes' include this assumption in your prerequisites. If not, add it to your outcomes. Figure 5.9 provides a highly comprehensive listing of learner prerequisites for a television technician training programme.

Prerequisites: television technician	
1	The learner must have the ability to use small machine and hand tools. Such tools include an electric drill, saw, pliers, hammer and chisels.
2	The learner must be able to read at the fifth-grade level.
3	The learner must be able to work in environments of extreme cold and hot climates. From −5° C to 40° C.
4	The learner must be physically fit and cannot have physical handicaps of the type that would restrict the learner from job duties. A learner must be able to work on the roofs of buildings without getting dizzy.
5	Assume knowledge of basic arithmetic operations, including addition, subtraction, multiplication and division.
6	The learner must be interested in working outdoors.
7	Normal colour vision is desirable, but not essential.

Figure 5.9   Examples: prerequisites for a programme to train a television technician

A similar approach can be used to define the prerequisites for a 'knowledge' package where no behavioural capabilities may be specified. Figure 5.10 is an example from a unit on 'Specifying learning outcomes', part of a programme on e-learning.

Of course pre-assessment may also reveal that some learners already possess some of the skills necessary to perform the behaviour to be learned. Where possible the programme should be structured to allow learners to go straight to the parts they need; see Chapter 6.

Assumed from previous knowledge	Explained in this unit
Performance analysis Goal-directed learning Cognitive learning Learning module	Performance standards Taxonomies Pre and post testing Learning gain

Figure 5.10   Prerequisites for a course on e-learning

CRITERIA FOR EFFECTIVE TESTS

In spending time on phrasing clear outcomes you will also have made your task of assessing them easier. Figure 5.11 summarizes four criteria for assessment tests.

Validity	The test must be an appropriate assessment of the capability described in the outcomes. A multiple-choice test would not be regarded as an appropriate method of assessing creative writing skills. Describing how to set up a machine is not the same as operating it. Sometimes it will be necessary to rely on an examiner's judgement. To ensure validity, the assessor must be given as much guidance as possible. (See Chapter 7.)
Range and number of questions	Test items should be based on the requirements specified in the outcomes. In our mortgage lending example six cases should offer a sufficient number of opportunities to test the learner's achievement of the outcome.
Nature of response	Think carefully how you would expect the learner to give their solutions to the problem. In the test for the mortgage loan programme the learner could be asked a question such as 'For each case say whether you make an advance or not'. But how exactly should they record their answers? This type of question could be presented in free response format but it would not be easy to anticipate all the likely responses, which could include a variety of terms synonymous with loan. A more simplistic approach would be to give the learner a binary choice – just clicking on Yes or No. But this might fail to adequately explore borderline cases. You might get round this by adding a third option such as More information required.
Acceptability	If a simulation of reality is used for the test it must be sufficiently robust and realistic not to alienate the learners. Learners also tend to be alienated by examples taken from other work environments or contexts. Even where the context is familiar the treatment may not be acceptable. A car manufacturer retraining engineers from other companies on a child's version of their flagship model found the experiment failed. Although the smaller version was identical, the adult trainees resented having to learn from it. For similar reasons multi-media programmes using cartoon characters need to be carefully piloted before general use.

Figure 5.11   Criteria for effective tests

In summary, a test should reflect the outcomes on which it is based. Suppose an outcome for a programme for the office staff of a mail order company requires them to make decisions about crediting agents' accounts for returned goods. A post-test question on this course such as 'State the rules for giving credit on returns' will be useful. But the test will surely be incomplete unless trainees are tested on specimen cases of agents' letters.

SUMMARY

- Learning outcomes (or 'objectives') describe the capabilities learners aim to acquire.
- Well defined outcomes benefit learners, trainers and management.
- Programme designers can prescribe outcomes for specific units or for a complete curriculum.
- Wherever possible the learning outcome should specify conditions and a standard of achievement.
- Clearly defined outcomes enable the effective design of tests.
- Tests may be used to diagnose readiness for learning as well as achievement.
- Tests should reflect the performance and standards described in the learning outcomes.

6 Making a Learning Plan

THIS CHAPTER WILL HELP YOU:

- analyse the content of your programme
- draw up a plan of the components that will make up the programme.

In Chapter 1 we suggested you should first analyse your learner group and then the content/skills that will form your programme. In this chapter we look at the analysis of content in more detail. We go on to consider how content might best be organized, to make the learner's job more manageable, and how the 'chunks' of learning (modules and sections) might be sequenced.

As we said in Chapter 1, the stages of planning an e-learning programme (see Figure 1.1, p. 2) are not mutually exclusive. The programme developer will customarily move to and fro between stages. For example, the outcomes may need revision as more is found out about the existing knowledge of the learner group.

Content analysis

This stage includes:

- a description of what is to be learned
- a breakdown of the learning into main areas and tasks
- links between the main areas and tasks.

This stage requires input from a learning designer, often known as a training or learning technologist. A word first about the way in which we are using the word 'technology'. The term is often taken to mean equipment and apparatus: projectors, television and above all computers. In this sense, a technologist would be expert in operating and troubleshooting such devices. In our view this is an inadequate definition – akin to believing that food technology is about cookers or soil technology about earth-moving machines. We define technology more broadly as the systematic application of organized knowledge to practical tasks.

Part of the job of the technologist is to bring to bear the most up-to-date and complete knowledge of how learning occurs, to design programmes that work. This includes:

- defining and recording all the terms, concepts, rules and procedures that comprise what has to be learned
- taking decisions about the size of each learning 'chunk' based on knowledge of the learner group as well as of the content to be learned
- taking decisions about the sequencing of the chunks
- advising on other aspects of the programme, such as the uses of different media, the layout of the materials, how learning might be managed electronically and what kinds of additional support learners might need (for example from a tutor).

The learning plan may be an analysis of content or skills, competence or activity based; we give a variety of examples in this chapter.

The learning may comprise a whole occupation or subject, such as car maintenance or chess, or it may consist of a quite specific skill or ability such as adjusting the brakes of a car or the 'en passant' play in chess. Two examples of the 'whole topic' variety are given in Figure 6.1A and B; two examples from more specific subjects are given in Figures 6.1C and D.

Retail selling is the process whereby a member of staff who normally works in a customer contact area assists shoppers in making purchases. This includes establishing and maintaining contact with customers in a positive and friendly manner. By the use of conversation involving questioning and listening the assistant will help the customer in the identification of their buying motives, using their knowledge of the product features, benefits and availability to help the customer make their decision. This may require the assistant to demonstrate or advise on technical factors and to reassure the customer where uncertainties arise or otherwise overcome customer objections if possible. The process is completed when the customer makes a decision to buy or otherwise concludes the interaction. In all cases the customer must be left satisfied with a favourable opinion of the company.

A   Topic synopsis: retail selling

Bridge is a card game played by two opposing pairs. The game has two major phases. In the first, bidding, a player attempts to agree with his partner a contract to win a number of tricks (seven or more) in each hand dealt. In the second phase the partnership bidding to the highest level attempts to win the contracted number of tricks. For every trick each player plays one of his 13 cards. The highest card played wins. In the bidding phase, since each player's cards are concealed, partnerships must have a system of evaluating hands and indicating their likely strength through the bids made. In play, it is important to remember the cards played and note other clues to the likely distribution of the opponent's cards.

B   Topic synopsis: bridge

The plug wirer is employed in the service department of a large department store which sells and repairs electrical equipment of all kinds. He connects plugs to the power leads of all new equipment and replaces faulty plugs on items returned for servicing and repair. The power leads are two- or three-core flexes coded to both the old and the new standards.

C   Job description: plug wirer

Passenger baggage must be checked at check-in in accordance with IATA regulations to meet the requirements of the airline's insurers.

Baggage is divided into two principal categories: items which accompany the passenger into the aircraft and those which go into the hold.

A charge is applied to those hold items which exceed the basic allowance. Check-in staff must calculate and process this payment.

D   Job description: checking passenger baggage

Figure 6.1   Examples of topic synopses

THE JOB/TOPIC BREAKDOWN

The learning plan structures the area of performance for which training is to be provided, as in Figure 6.2.

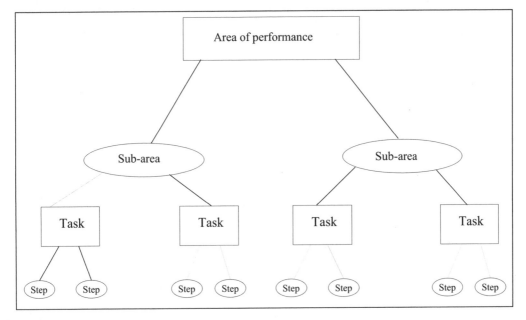

Figure 6.2   Breaking down performance (after Harless 1975)

Most procedures of any reasonable scope will divide into sub-areas. Within each sub-area you will usually find a number of tasks. Figure 6.3 shows the breakdown for the topic of bridge. This may at first sight appear rather esoteric. However, bridge has the virtue of comprising the teaching of a wide range of learning types including procedures, simple and more advanced concepts and problem-solving strategies. Bridge sub-divides into four main sub-areas; later we consider the further division of these into tasks.

Figure 6.4 applies the same technique to the job of airline staff who deal with passengers on the ground. There are three sub-areas. We have shown how one of these sub-divides into four tasks. One of these tasks in turn sub-divides into a number of steps.

In the case of a smaller topic you may only have a couple of sub-areas or none at all. 'Setting up a micro-computer', for example would have two sub-areas, 'Connecting the components' and 'Booting the system'.

SPECIFYING TASKS

In the example of bridge we can see that the simplest sub-area, preparing to play, comprises two basic tasks 'Deciding the dealer' and 'Dealing'. In the case of 'Setting up a computer' two tasks within the sub-area 'Connecting components' would be 'Adjusting the monitor' and 'Identifying cables'.

Training designers can adapt this sort of model to particular circumstances. Sometimes a fairly complex task is easier to break down if the steps are grouped rather than listed sequen-

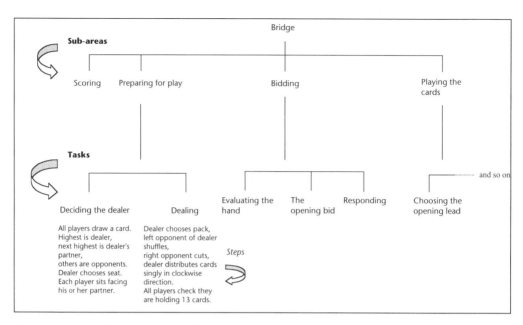

Figure 6.3   Topic breakdown for bridge

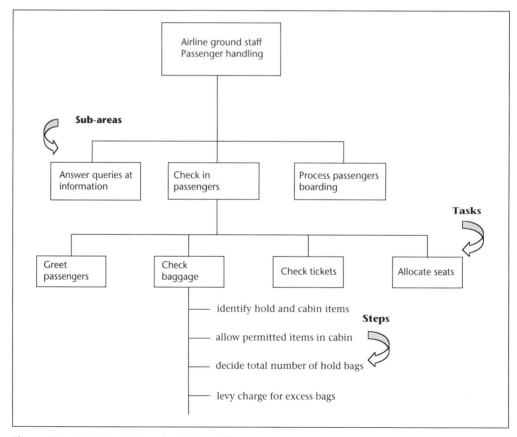

Figure 6.4   Topic breakdown for airline staff

tially. Figure 6.5 illustrates how the task of wiring a plug has been first sub-divided into three sub-tasks or components. The steps comprising each sub-task are then grouped.

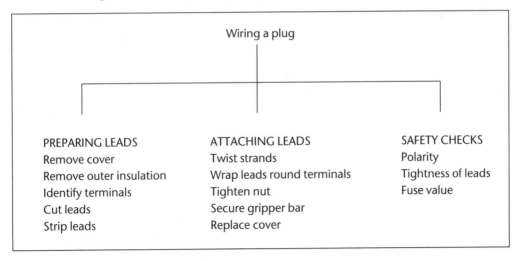

Figure 6.5   Topic breakdown for wiring a plug

ANALYSING MORE GENERAL TOPICS

The same strategy can also be applied to the analysis of more general topics. Suppose we need to prepare a learning programme on basic management skills. Figure 6.6 shows a possible breakdown.

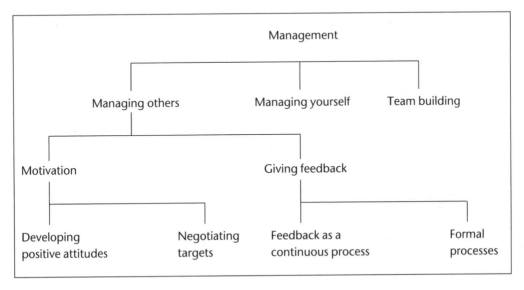

Figure 6.6   Topic breakdown for a general subject

Designing a modular structure

The designer is now in a position to:

• decide on the size of each 'chunk' of learning
• decide on the sequence in which the learners will study these chunks.

We pointed out in Chapter 1 that the best way to think of the size of a chunk is to use learner hours: how long will it take an average learner to study the chunk? We showed how a programme might be broken down into 'blocks', then 'modules' and then 'sections' (sometimes other terms are used, for example 'unit') (see Figure 6.7).

In developing a modular plan a rough guide is to relate modules to tasks. Until recently a module would typically comprise one or two sections, each of 30–40 minutes learning time. The growing interest in desktop learning and electronic performance support systems (EPSS) has been accompanied by the development of shorter sessions of 15 or even 10 minutes

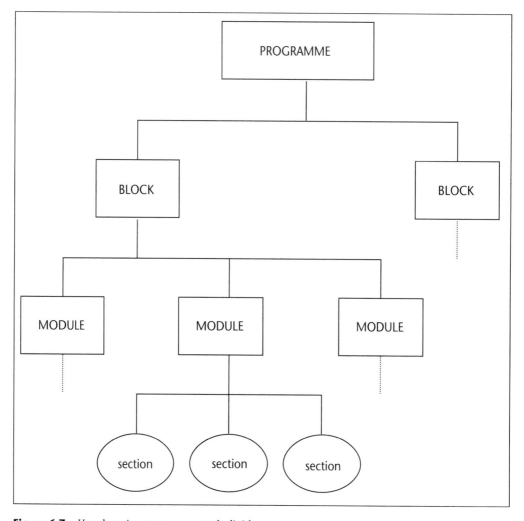

Figure 6.7   How learning programmes sub-divide

duration that focus on very specific tasks. Taking such a section is like accessing the HELP function in Microsoft Word.

In a package comprising printed text, particularly for management and communications topics, modules tend to be of longer duration, say up to two hours. In a large package several modules may be grouped into blocks relating to the sub-areas or tasks of your content analysis. So for bridge 'The opening bid' alone might require two or three sections. On the other hand, 'Wiring a plug', though comprising three sub-tasks, may be covered in one section.

WHAT SHOULD BE IN YOUR PLAN?

When you look at the task level in your job/topic breakdown a modular structure will usually suggest itself readily enough. In the case of bridge several of the task level items convert easily to sections, for example 'Evaluating the hand' and 'Choosing the opening lead'.

But the task–module approach will not work in every case. In bridge some trivial tasks can be easily combined into a single module. Thus the two tasks which comprise the sub-area 'Preparing for play' would form a quite brief section even if combined. Conversely 'Responding' will need two or more sections as it involves a number of complex concepts.

Example 1: Bridge

Figure 6.8 demonstrates how a whole module (A2) is devoted to just one aspect of the bidding process in the game of bridge. As many as four or five modules may be required to cover the topic fully. In Module A1 you will see that the hand evaluation task has been combined with another task – selecting the opening bid. Hand evaluation is a simple arithmetical procedure and does not warrant separate treatment. Note that in our bridge example the assumption is that the package will stand alone. If we were to make provision for some form of tutorial support we should need a fifth column headed 'tutor role' or similar.

Module	Scope	Learning outcomes	Duration
A1	Hand evaluation: opening bid as dealer	a) Evaluate a selection of hands according to point-count and honour-trick systems	20 minutes
		b) As dealer select an opening bid for a selection of hands of 11 to 15 points, no hand having more than one five-card suit	40–60 minutes
A2	Respond to opening bids of 1	For a selection of hands respond to partner's opening bid by passing or bidding	40–60 minutes

Figure 6.8   Provisional learning plan for the package on bridge

Example 2: Management

In this topic you will not be teaching linear procedures and each module may cover a number of tasks and concepts. An inspection of the breakdown of this topic in Figure 6.6 suggests that the two components of motivation and giving feedback may become four learning sections as follows:

- Section 1A Motivation: developing positive attitudes
- Section 1B Motivation: negotiating targets
- Section 2A Giving feedback: the continuous process
- Section 2B Giving feedback: the formal process

MODULAR SCHEDULING AND LEARNER DIVERSITY

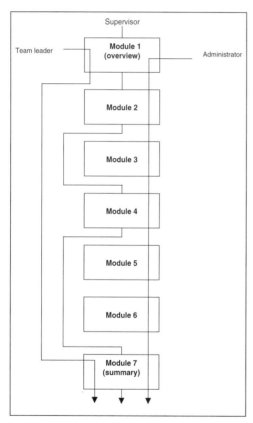

A modular structure enables the training designer to take account of differences in employee experience and work responsibilities. A well-structured learning programme can accommodate several levels of trainee. Figure 6.9 shows the sort of progress a team leader, supervisor and administrator respectively might make through a unit of seven modules. Although it is possible for the more experienced people to skip material that they know already the sequence is essentially linear.

For certain topics a linear path is unavoidable. You can't learn dividing before subtracting. But often a topic will include concepts that are not directly interdependent. You can learn them – or some of them – in any order. Figure 6.10 is the modular plan for a learning programme on learning outcomes and tests. After Module 2 learners can choose to take Module 3 or 4. If they choose 4 they must next take 5 and 6 in either order. They can then take Module 3 before completing the programme with Module 7. The more opportunities you can devise for this type of choice the more attractive the material will be to the learner.

Figure 6.9   Progress through a sequence of modules

Your work in specifying and sequencing content will inevitably prompt decisions in two other areas:

- the design and layout of the material
- the nature of any tutorial or other support you will need to provide for learners.

These areas are covered in Chapters 8, 9 and 10.

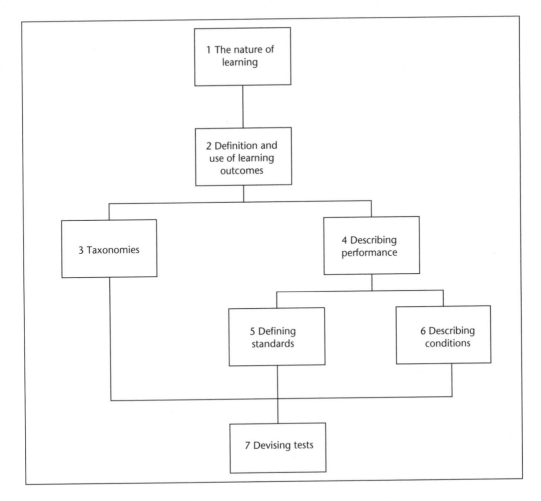

Figure 6.10   Modular scheme for a programme on learning outcomes and tests

SUMMARY

● ●

- The subject matter or capability that is to be learned can be divided and sub-divided into different levels of detail.
- This analytical process makes it easier to identify the 'chunks' into which to divide the learning programme.
- Learning programmes may often be divided into three levels – blocks, modules and sections or units.
- A section (or 'unit') would typically have a duration of 20–40 minutes.
- Modules and sections/units are identified from the task level of the subject-matter breakdown.
- A modular plan gives the outcomes, duration and delivery mode for each module and its component units or sections.
- Learners should be helped to study only those modules (or parts of them) that they require.

7 Managing Assessment

THIS CHAPTER WILL HELP YOU:

- justify the importance of assessment in e-learning
- identify points in the programme at which assessment is needed
- use criteria for evaluating assessment tests
- ensure electronic assessment works smoothly
- use the results of assessment to improve the programme.

The importance of assessment in e-learning

Assessment entails making judgements about people. In a learning context these judgements are made about the extent to which individuals achieve the stated outcomes of the programme. Hence another term commonly used to describe this process is 'achievement testing'. In e-learning the tests are often taken on a computer but this will not always be the case, particularly for 'soft' skills (such as communicating with people) or manual skills (such as operating equipment). It is also important to remember that not all electronic assessment is instantaneous, for example a tutor may be needed to 'mark' a report submitted electronically and the speed of that will depend on his or her availability.

This is a typical sequence of computer assessment:

- The computer displays a question or problem, often the first of a series (Figure 7.1A).
- The learner responds by typing, clicking, touching the screen. (Figure 7.1B).
- The computer confirms the correctness of the answer, that is, the learner receives feedback on their progress (Figure 7.1C).

A

Effective English for Business Letters   *Getting the meaning right*

Three sentences follow that may contain some common mistakes with word selection. In each sentence one or more words have been used incorrectly because they sound like the correct word.

Here's the first sentence. Please type the correct word(s) for each sentence, then press ENTER.

'A great deal of time was expanded on his violin practise.'

[   ]

B

Effective English for Business Letters	*Getting the meaning right*

Three sentences follow that may contain some common mistakes with word selection. In each sentence one or more words have been used incorrectly because they sound like the correct word.

Here's the first sentence. Please type the correct word(s) for each sentence, then press ENTER.

'A great deal of time was expanded on his violin practise.'

practice	

C

Effective English for Business Letters	*Getting the meaning right*

Three sentences follow that may contain some common mistakes with word selection. In each sentence one or more words have been used incorrectly because they sound like the correct word.

Here's the first sentence. Please type the correct word(s) for each sentence, then press ENTER.

'A great deal of time was expanded on his violin practise.'

practice	

Yes, 'practise' is wrong – it's a verb; but you missed 'expanded' which means to grow in size. The correct use should be 'expended'.

Figure 7.1   A typical sequence of computer assessment

WHY ASSESS?

Figure 7.2 shows several reasons for assessing learners' performance. Note that assessment helps all the stakeholders: learners, employers, sponsors and programme managers.

THE RANGE OF ASSESSMENT

Assessment methods vary. The chief factor affecting choice of method is the nature of the learning outcomes.

Some topics and skills can be assessed by standard marking systems such as multiple-choice questions. Others require human assessors to make judgements. Figure 7.3 gives some idea of the range of methods you might need to use.

Reason for assessment	Comment
To give learners feedback on progress	We like to know how well we have learned a new skill. And we need to know as we go. For many skills, such as cookery, the answer is obvious. But if we have made a mistake in applying the new skill we often need help getting it right – ask any golfer. The closer the feedback to the practice, the better. In asynchronous forms of e-learning there is the risk that feedback might be delayed longer than is desirable.
To help learners follow the most effective route through the programme	Learning programmes are often divided and sub-divided into modules and sections or units (see Chapter 6). Since no two learners have exactly the same knowledge about a topic, or learn at the same rate, it is usually desirable to help them find their individual routes through the programme. Assessment can help learners select the sequence of study most suited to their personal needs.
To make the learning credible to employers	Formal assessment results and qualifications reassure employers and others who need evidence of competence.
To enable people to gain qualifications	Formal evidence of their new capabilities also helps the learner. Certificates and other types of accreditation help learners build credits towards higher level skills, are useful in career development and help develop self-esteem. Some form of assessment is essential if learning is to be certificated.
To enable sponsors to verify the effectiveness of the learning	Those responsible for funding the development of learning programmes and of paying student fees (for example employers and parents) need to know whether they are getting value for money. Assessment helps sponsors verify that the learning outcomes are being achieved – by the expected numbers of learners and to the appropriate standard.
To improve the learning programme	Assessment information helps managers and designers identify those parts of the programme that are giving difficulty. Problematic sections can be rewritten taking account of the performance of the learners who have used the programme so far.

Figure 7.2   Reasons for assessment

Skill type	Example/s	Assessment method/s
Interactive 'people' skills	Discussing, listening, explaining (one-to-one and group)	Tutor assessed role play (possibly synchronous e-learning), ongoing assessment in work-based learning context
Planning/problem solving	Scheduling time and resources for a project	Project plan including Gantt chart
One-way written communications	Writing letters and reports	Workbook exercises with feedback within the learning programme, portfolio (including online activities) assessed by tutor
Number skills	Calculating, estimating, data handling	Online exercises and workbook
Physical skills	Operating a machine, carrying out manual processes	Assessment by expert

Figure 7.3   Assessment methods

CASE STUDY: ASYNCHRONOUS LEARNING

The e-journal *Asynchronous Learning Networks* (*JALN*) describes an online course taught at Vanderbilt University on the topic of asynchronous learning (Bourne *et al.* 1997).

The course was designed to explore a number of research questions such as:

- How important/useful are face-to-face sessions?
- How does use of web conferencing affect student use of e-mail?
- How popular is peer-to-peer learning? Will it increase?
- Does the use of mentors improve effectiveness?

The course used a number of assessment methods including:

- project work in small groups
- individual and group assignments
- questionnaires
- portfolios of completed work
- contributions to conferences and the help given to other learners
- use (by individuals and teams) of websites and website features
- online pre- and post-tests using multiple choice questions.

When assessment takes place

Assessment can occur at various stages during learning:

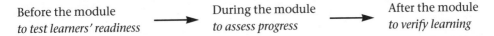

Before the module
to test learners' readiness

During the module
to assess progress

After the module
to verify learning

The three types of assessment are usually labelled 'diagnostic', 'formative' and 'summative', reflecting their different purposes and emphases. Figure 7.4 (an extended version of Figure 5.8) shows how learners might pass through each of these stages.

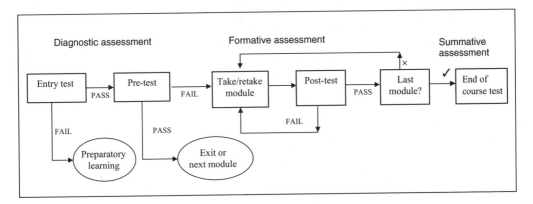

Figure 7.4   The stages of assessment

DIAGNOSTIC ASSESSMENT

We discussed the entry test and the pre-entry test in Chapter 5. These are diagnostic in that they seek to establish what the learner already knows and can do, and to help the learner find the best route towards achieving the outcomes. Certain pre-knowledge might be essential, for example a basic skills learner could not begin a module on long division before mastering multiplication. Thus, as the diagram suggests, we may decide to assess learners on their readiness to start the programme in an entry test. At this stage we are asking if the learner is ready to start the programme: do they possess the prerequisite knowledge and skills? If the answer is 'No', then, as the diagram suggests, we may arrange some preparatory learning.

The pre-test offers a different form of diagnostic assessment, designed for use at the module level (Figure 7.5). It seeks to answer the question: 'Does this learner *need* to study this module?' Many learners complain of boredom induced by being presented with too much material that they know already. The pre-test aims to avoid such redundancy.

FORMATIVE ASSESSMENT

Formative assessment takes place as the learner works through their programme. It can:

- identify difficulties the learner is having as they arise
- determine reasons for these difficulties
- help the learner resolve them.

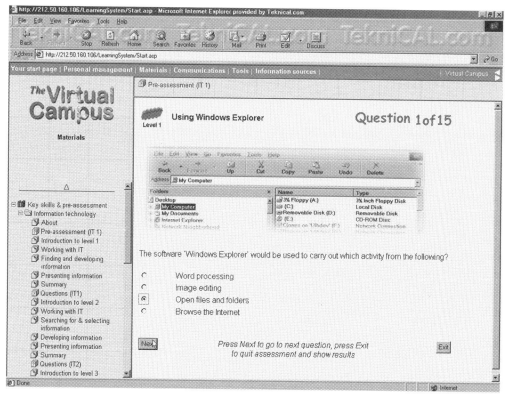

Figure 7.5   A diagnostic question from an online programme

In all these ways formative assessment can help the learner; its purpose is to make learning more effective.

There are two levels of formative assessment: assessment points along the way and a post test at the end (Figure 7.6). The figure shows the learner's progress through an e-learning module of, say, 20 minutes. At each of the three assessment points a review tests the learner's mastery of the content covered so far. At the end of the module the post-test assesses their grasp of the entire content of the module. Assessment points can review understanding of the smallest discrete elements of the programme – the learning steps. For each step the learning designer will explain the new concept, procedure or skill to be learned, illustrating it with worked examples. Each of the assessment points will prepare the learner to answer a similar question in the post-test for that module.

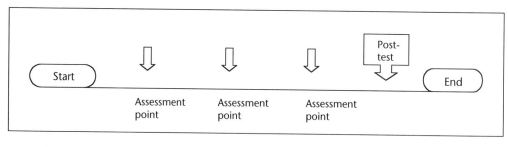

Figure 7.6   Formative assessment in learning modules

Formative assessment at the learning step level will not only require the learner to solve a problem or answer a question; it will also provide feedback as we saw in the example earlier in this chapter. To be useful, the feedback will be prompt (hence the value of electronic feedback, which is usually instantaneous). It will also need to be detailed enough to guide the learner as to their next steps and it will need to be clearly expressed. An assessment point is a stage in the learning process. The cumulative effect of the assessment points in a module is to consolidate the learner's acquisition of new knowledge and skills.

The post-test at the end of the module is designed to verify that the learner has achieved the outcomes for that module. Here learning tends to give way to verification. The post-test helps:

- learners to confirm the progress that they are making and plan their future learning
- tutors to identify areas of the topic where further help may be necessary
- authors to identify aspects of the programme that may need rewriting
- managers to check the effectiveness of the programme.

We have included the post-test in our section on formative assessment. This is because we are assuming that it is testing learner achievement on a single module rather than achievement on the whole programme. The distinguishing characteristic of formative assessment is that it provides learners with feedback on their learning, enabling them to take action accordingly. To do this, it has to provide feedback as well as a comment or mark. If no feedback is provided, the post-test becomes an example of summative assessment, which we look at in the next section.

SUMMATIVE ASSESSMENT

Summative assessment measures the extent to which the learner has achieved the outcomes of the programme and acquired new capabilities and knowledge. Its main purpose is not to provide detailed feedback to the learner but to make a final judgement, for example:

- to enable learners to receive accreditation (such as a certificate)
- to assess the learner's suitability for promotion
- to provide a licence to practise
- to demonstrate the organization's skill level to customers
- to enable management to verify the success of the training strategy.

To achieve these outcomes summative assessment has to meet a number of criteria. It has to be open and transparent, so that everyone (and especially the learner) has access to, and understands, the 'rules of the game'. This covers not only the clarity of the instructions of assessment questions but also such matters as cut-off dates for submission and arrangements for appealing against a result. Figure 7.7 shows how summative assessment may be given in an online course. Arrangements for summative assessment also have to be secure – we look at that later. But the two main criteria summative assessment has to meet are validity and reliability and we consider these next.

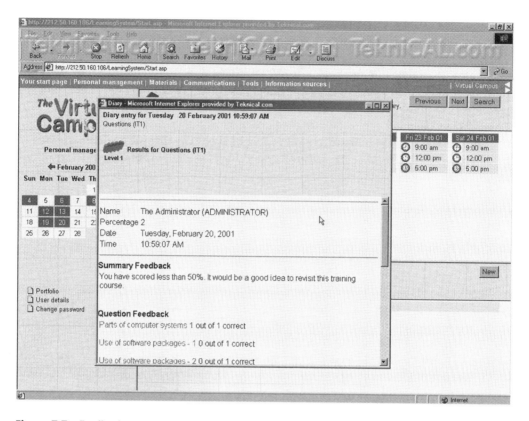

Figure 7.7   Feedback on summative assessment

Criteria for evaluating assessment

People often complain that a test or examination was 'not fair'. In their perception it did not treat all the learners even-handedly or it contained questions or problems that were confusing or ambiguous. Such complaints suggest that the assessment is 'invalid' or 'unreliable'.

VALIDITY

A test or examination is said to be valid when it measures what it claims to measure and when what is measured is clearly significant. Thus a module requiring learners to use a word-processing program to edit a letter could validly present a number of different letters and ask learners to edit these to a defined standard. But, as we have seen, it is not always as easy to achieve validity in assessment in e-learning, for example when learners are seeking to develop interpersonal or physical skills. In these cases, to be valid at least some of the assessment will have to be carried out away from the computer.

Validity has a number of aspects, as set out in Figure 7.8.

Aspect of validity	Example
The learning outcome must be worth achieving, worthwhile (rather than irrelevant or trivial).	In a module on the use of a calculator to solve problems, learning the names and functions of the keys would be insufficient.
The assessment arrangements must be credible to learners and other stakeholders; this includes the method of assessment, the people/system carrying it out, and the number and variety of test items.	In a module on airline destinations for baggage handlers (for example LHR=London Heathrow) two or three assessment items would be insufficient. In a module on mortgage lending for building society staff a mixture of cases would be needed, including individuals and families, seeking loans across the social and geographical spectrum.
The method used must be an appropriate way of assessing the performance and predicting future competence.	A module on hairdressing should at some point require performance in a busy salon.

Figure 7.8   Aspects of validity

Example

In an induction course new sales staff in a department store are assessed on the following outcomes.

At the end of Module 2 you should be able to:

- label with their correct names pictures of the founding partners of the company
- give the birth and death dates of each of the founding partners
- state the address of the first shop the company opened
- give the date on which the first shop was destroyed by fire.

Assessment of their ability to retain such background information would be unlikely to help sales staff function effectively in their key tasks soon after appointment.

A SYSTEM FOR CLASSIFYING LEARNING OUTCOMES

Dating from the 1950s and still one of the most useful handbooks on classifying learning content is the *Taxonomy of Educational Objectives – The Classification of Educational Goals*, produced by a committee of American educational researchers and edited by B.S. Bloom (Bloom *et al.* 1964). The stimulus for the publication was a widespread feeling among US college examiners that their methods of assessment were imprecise. The committee felt that examiners were confused about the nature of educational outcomes and how to express them. What was needed was a common assessment methodology. The committee agreed that the theoretical framework they were seeking 'might best be obtained through a system of classifying the goals of the educational process, since educational objectives provide the basis for building curricula and tests''

At the macro level Bloom's committee classified outcomes or objectives into three main areas or domains. These are shown in Figure 7.9. As Bloom pointed out, the cognitive domain 'is most central to the work of much current test development'. This domain has six categories of outcome, as set out in Figure 7.10, with examples.

Domain	Description	Example/s
Cognitive domain	Objectives that deal with recall or recognition; use of intellectual abilities and skills	Interpreting statistical graphs Making calculations Evaluating alternative courses of action
Affective domain	Objectives that describe interests, attitudes and values, and the development of appreciation	Developing and prioritizing values of importance to the individual Art appreciation
Psychomotor domain	Objectives relating to manipulative or motor skills	Driving a car Using apparatus

Figure 7.9   A system for classifying learning outcomes

Levels of the cognitive domain	Description	Example/s
Knowledge	Recall of specifics, knowledge of theories	List the levels of Maslow's hierarchy In your own words state Ohm's law
Comprehension	Translating, interpreting, and so on	According to the balance sheets which company is doing better? What does *force majeure* mean?
Application	Applying theories and concepts to cases	Write a learning outcome for the following task Draw up a spreadsheet for a project
Analysis	Demonstrating the relationships of parts of a whole	Underline the verbs in this sentence Draw an organization chart of your company
Synthesis	Creating new structures	Design an e-learning package for a new appraisal scheme
Evaluation	Using criteria to judge value	Devise and use a rating sheet to assess an e-learning tutor

Figure 7.10   A classification of types of cognitive learning

Example

The following example is of a test on the application of financial principles. Table 7.1 shows the constituent topics in the left-hand column, together with the cognitive levels at which testing will apply. The examiner has decided to test at three levels: recall (level 1), application (level 3) and analysis (level 4).

Table 7.1   Assessment at different levels

| Topics | Abilities | | | |
	Recall	Application	Analysis	Total (%)
Production	5	3	2	10
Banking & money	12	8	10	30
International trade	11	8	6	25
Population	4	3	3	10
Public finance	14	7	4	25
Total	46	29	25	100

The high percentage of recall questions suggests the test is not valid. The programme seeks to help people *apply* the principles of finance but nearly 50 per cent of the score is for simple recall. Some of the level 1 questions could almost certainly have been upgraded to levels 2 or 3, for example by requiring the learner to interpret tables and diagrams.

RELIABILITY

Assessment methods must also be reliable, producing consistent results every time. A 'reliable' assessor makes the same decision on every occasion; if there are several assessors then all should come to the same judgement on a learner's work. This is an ideal: in reality, assessment is rarely totally reliable though, as we shall see, you can work to improve reliability. Automated assessment is more likely to be reliable but (and this can be a big but) this can be at the expense of validity.

The assessment method most likely to produce reliability in testing is the objective test. An objective test contains questions to which there is a single, unambiguous answer. The multiple-choice question is the most popular form of objective test in both paper-based and computer-based assessment systems. These tests are well-suited to the assessment of knowledge but they can also be used to assess some skills.

The University of East Anglia suggests that even at higher levels than recall, computer-assisted assessment is usually more reliable and consistent than paper-based approaches since it uses one set of pre-programmed rules to assess scripts. It is also more efficient in that the checks needed to ensure consistency across a team of human examiners are redundant.

Example: word-processing

Electronic testing of word-processing can be simple. Candidates can be asked to print a document or set tasks involving cutting and pasting. More complex testing can require the candidate to edit a document from handwritten amendment to draft. Their answer is then compared with a model answer. Assessment criteria enable the errors to be identified and classified into different types.

While not 100 per cent objective, such tests can be carried out with a high degree of reliability in electronic form, particularly as there is no limit to the number of examples that can be given. The larger the number of exercises the learner undertakes, the more reliable the result.

Humans and computers are stronger in different areas. Research carried out by UEA found that human assessors are poor at discovering errors but good at classifying them whereas computers are good at finding errors but poor at classifying them. Computers cannot apply the 'common-sense' interpretation of assessment criteria that the experienced human assessor brings to bear. The solution suggested by the researchers is to combine assessment methods: the automated assessor deals with errors where classification is simple, leaving the human examiner to evaluate the less clear-cut cases. The report observes that for word-processing assessment approximately 90 per cent of scripts were processed by computer while the remaining 10 per cent were passed to human assessors. Relatively small changes to assessment criteria could have reduced the numbers passed to human assessment to 5 per cent.

Improving reliability with human assessors

While computers play an important role in the assessment process, many types of assessment require judgements to be made by human assessors. In higher education such judgements often entail assessing written responses such as essays or reports. In business the assessor may evaluate the learner's ability to react in a scenario such as a role play or to comment on a case study. Judgements by assessors in such situations can vary enormously. Thus it is clearly important to devise an assessment method that makes it more likely that all learners are treated even-handedly whoever does the assessing. This is especially important in e-learning, when tutors may be working in isolation from one another, marking assignments they have not themselves set.

For those e-learning managers who will need to employ human assessment as well as electronic the following checklist may be useful:

CHECKLIST:

Prepare a systematic statement of learning outcomes for all units.
Produce a marking guide.
Run an exercise in which assessors agree on how to interpret the marking guide.
Brief all assessors on the process before assessment begins.
Hold frequent review meetings of assessors (by electronic conferencing).
Involve assessors in 'blind testing' of papers to compare standards and define criteria.
Make available samples from previous assessments.
Keep summative assessments to the minimum.
Brief students as well as assessors, so they too are clear about the criteria on which their work will be judged.

Portfolio assessment

Some assessment can proceed wholly electronically but, as we have seen, some skills are not easily amenable to assessment by this means. This applies to most learning in the psychomotor and affective domains or where individuals or groups of learners are asked to carry out projects or to submit reports. Also, in recent years interest has grown amongst e-learning practitioners in what is known as collaborative learning: two or more learners undertaking activities and submitting a joint solution. In these cases, a variety of assessment methods is needed to secure validity. The methods will produce different kinds of evidence: reports, notes on a group work session, e-mails, project plans. Here a useful approach is portfolio assessment, which enables the learner to present a range of evidence gathered through the different assessment tasks.

First let us be clear about terminology. One school of thought defines an electronic portfolio as a computer-based form of a curriculum vitae: 'a webpage that highlights your abilities, achievements and intellect' (University of Pennsylvania, <www.upenn.edu/careerservices>). Our interest, however, is in the portfolio as a means of assessing learning. The portfolio is a record of the contributions that the learner has made to the programme throughout its duration. These may be activities that they have undertaken individually or in collaboration with their peers. A portfolio may be used for continuous assessment throughout a course but is more likely to be one of the tools of summative assessment.

One would expect that the portfolio submitted in an online course would itself be produced in electronic format, as a file or folder. This is often the case but sometimes it is easier and more appropriate to submit the portfolio as hard copy. Whether electronic or hard copy, the effective portfolio:

- reflects the outcomes of the programme
- is clearly organized, with logical sections
- numbers and dates all documents
- contains a table or map of contents
- is complete
- links the evidence to the programme outcomes and their assessment criteria
- provides evidence that the work is that of the person submitting it
- is easy to download (if in electronic form).

Effective electronic assessment

Research carried out by the University of East Anglia (Dowsing, Long and Craven 2000) identified four criteria for determining the effectiveness of electronic assessment:

- cost-effectiveness
- consistency, accuracy and reliability in assessment
- integration with existing methods
- acceptability to learners.

Effective electronic assessment brings a number of benefits:

- speed and consistency (through automating paper-based procedures)
- greater efficiency in storing, manipulating and transmitting data
- ease in monitoring progress
- flexibility in the timing of assessment
- greater sophistication in administering tests, for example via the use of the facility to generate questions randomly
- immediacy of feedback to the learner.

Assessment results can also be used to improve the learning programme itself. In some universities tutors are provided with exam results and a question analyis report. They can use these data to review how well learners have responded to the questions. The analysis includes a measure of how well each question discriminated between the strongest and weakest students, as shown in Figure 7.11. The bars in the chart show the responses by ranked ability groupings. Bar 1 gives the score of the 'best' fifth of the students. Bar 2 that of the next best fifth and so on. The analysis compares student scores for each question with their overall score.

Management issues

Assessment in e-learning programmes poses a number of challenges to managers. These include the need to:

- ensure security, whilst safeguarding the learner's privacy
- manage the assessment of practical or interpersonal skills
- ensure assessment arrangements are piloted and monitored once in operation
- ensure that all assessment arrangements are clear to participants (especially to tutors and learners).

SECURITY IN ASSESSMENT

There are four aspects to the security of information:

- confidentiality (knowing that the information has not been read by a third party)
- authentication (knowing that the information has, in fact, come from the person who claims to have sent it)
- integrity (knowing that the information has not been corrupted in transit)
- non-repudiation (knowing that the sender of the information cannot later deny having sent it).

Various tools are available to ensure maximum security in electronic assessment. One option is to use a smart card which is, in effect, a miniature computer. Smart cards are used by a number of universities and businesses. A single card can be used to identify the bearer, process financial transactions, gain access to premises, keep records of library loans and search databases.

The card reader/writers for contact cards are relatively simple devices. The card is inserted until contact is made with the standard interface and the relevant data is read. Readers can be attached to personal computers through standard interfaces such as serial ports or via a modem. They can also be stand alone. Depending on the level of security the

Correct answer E. Discrimination 0.60

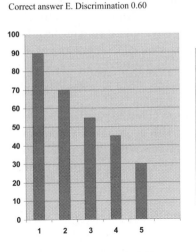

The majority of students (71%)
chose the correct response.
Although three of the distractors
attracted very little attention the
bars "stepping down" from left to
right are an indication of good
discrimination. The graph
indicates that 90% of the top fifth
of students answered this question
correctly (column 1), 70% of the
'next best ' with only 30% of the
least able students answering
correctly.

Correct answer D. Discrimination 0.55

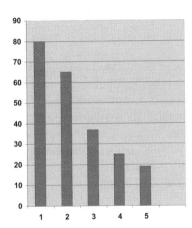

In this case the responses are
more evenly spread out. Note that
only 45% of all the students
answered correctly; the other
responses are shared among the
distractors. The discrimination of
0.55 indicates that this is a good
question and the graph again steps
down from left to right where the
responses by ranked ability
groupings are 80%; 65%; 37%;
25% and 19%.

Correct answer: E. Discrimination 0.00

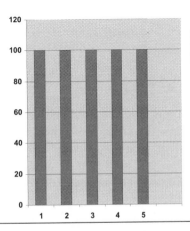

Some would say that this is not a
good question as there is no
discrimination – everybody got
this question right. It can be
argued that it would make a good
first question – in order to build
up confidence. Some designers
like to include a few easy
questions at the start of a paper
which the majority of students
can answer correctly so as to help
them get started.

Figure 7.11   Discrimination analysis of examination questions
(reproduced by kind permission of the University of Northumbria at Newcastle)

user may have to key in their personal identification number (PIN). There is considerable flexibility as to the components that can be configured into a smart card reader/writer.

Additional security can be incorporated by having dual-card readers. This can be important, for example, in medical applications where some of the data should only be made available to a doctor or to a pharmacist. In these cases a valid doctor's card or pharmacist's card would have to be inserted into the second slot and authenticated before the relevant information was made available.

A smart card enables the cardholder to be quickly and clearly identified. A form of 'electronic signature' is a requirement to this end. This could take the form of basic details (for example names, birth date, etc.) or, if higher security is required, a PIN number or biometric. A biometric is a means of physical identification such as a photograph or fingerprint.

Smart cards can:

- have tamper resistant architecture built into the hardware. If the card is tampered with the information held in the chip will automatically be destroyed.
- be manufactured with a photograph of the owner so that a visual check can be made to ensure that the presenter is, in fact, the authorized user.
- provide different levels of security access using different passwords, PIN numbers or cryptography.

The smart card can be programmed to carry out sophisticated and rapid data encryption and decryption. Encryption transforms information that is stored on the card into an unreadable format according to specific rules. When the information is deciphered it is restored to its original format. This is the decryption process. Only those who have a secret key can decrypt the information. There are a number of different standards and it is naturally an area that has been very extensively researched because of the importance of financial applications of smart cards. Modern cryptographic standards are very difficult to break.

Protection for an individual by having one piece of information that is uniquely theirs can only be ensured with a biometric that can be stored on the individual's card. For example fingerprint recognition systems are commercially available from leading manufacturers. Finger imaging biometrics is developing as a highly secure method of tying a card to a specific individual. A recent innovation in one UK financial institution is to use the unique 'eyeprint' of an individual as the means of authentication.

Most issues relating to personal privacy and smart cards are covered by the Data Protection Act 1984.

MANAGING ASSESSMENT OF PRACTICAL SKILLS

We have pointed out that, on many programmes, you will need to use forms of assessment that measure practical or interpersonal skills – the kinds of performance it is difficult or impossible to assess validly by electronic means. You may in these circumstances need to organize face-to-face assessment activities. You will need to book an appropriate location (with parking) and ensure access (including for disabled learners). You will also need to brief assessors and admininstrators.

PILOTING ASSESSMENT ARRANGEMENTS

As we pointed out in Chapter 2, all aspects of a new e-learning programme need to be piloted. This applies to assessment. You can gauge the effectiveness of assessment by looking at the results (see the example from Newcastle given) and by asking tutors and learners for their views. Once the programme is operational these sources will help you monitor the continued effectiveness of assessment and make any necessary changes.

CLARITY OF ASSESSMENT

We have stressed the importance of clarity in all aspects of assessment. This begins right back with formulating the learning outcomes; clear outcomes make it easy to define the criteria for effective learner performance and this in turn helps you explain to learners exactly what is required of them, and to brief tutors. You need to ensure that assessment instructions are clear, including any word length requirements, how marks will be allocated and when and how learners should submit their work. Marking instructions also need to be clear to tutors, who are likely to be geographically separate from one another and who will not (unlike in conventional education or training) have set the assessments themselves.

SUMMARY

- Assessment helps all stakeholders in a learning programme, including the learners themselves, the programme developers and managers and those who sponsor the learning.
- Assessment methods vary depending on the type of skill being learned; electronic methods are not appropriate for every type of assessment.
- Assessment is used to assess readiness for learning, to check progress (formative assessment) and to verify achievement (summative assessment).
- Assessment methods may be evaluated according to a number of criteria but most commonly for the validity and reliability of the assessment.
- The reliability of human assessors can be improved by applying guidelines.
- Portfolios may be submitted online but should meet explicit criteria.
- Electronic assessment must be cost-effective, consistent, integrated with existing methods and acceptable to learners.
- The e-learning manager is responsible for the administration and security of electronic assessment methods.

8 Managing Learner Support

THIS CHAPTER WILL HELP YOU:

- identify the kinds of support e-learners need at different stages in their programme
- decide what support you need to provide in addition to the materials
- decide who can provide this support
- anticipate the expectations learners will have and how to address these
- identify any skills needed by tutors and other people who support learners
- select, induct, train and monitor tutorial and other support staff.

When people think of e-learning they tend to think largely of programme content: the capacity of technology to store and transmit seemingly endless amounts of information. But individuals need much more than information. When faced with learning something new they also need:

- the motivation to get started and then maintain momentum
- clear outcomes, so they know what they are aiming at and can recognize when they have achieved it
- opportunities to practise and get feedback on how they are doing.

To some extent, these kinds of support can be provided in the learning material, as shown in Figure 8.1. But materials are rarely enough; and reports of the failure of online

Support	Materials
Motivation	Sections linking content to learners' experiences, job prospects, etc.
Continuing interest	Careful structuring of material; use of illustrations, examples and anecdotes; user-friendly style with clear, short sentences
Clear outcomes	Outcomes worded in language that makes sense to learners and which is related to their experiences and aspirations
Opportunities to practise	Exercises, activities, questions, projects, case studies
Feedback	Answers to questions/exercises, checklists to help learners assess the results of projects/case studies

Figure 8.1   Support in the learning material

programmes to maintain learners' interest are now beginning to appear in the training press:

> [Some say] the problem is not with the students but with the courses, which cannot offer the face-to-face interaction needed to keep students interested. Experts say distance learning professors need to form personal ties to students.
>
> (*Chronicle of Higher Education*, February 2000)

The reason for student disappointment is linked to a failure to provide sufficient support in addition to that contained in the learning materials. We are talking about the electronic equivalent of the help a good face-to-face trainer would provide, for example:

- speaking individually to each learner
- answering their questions and responding to their particular problems
- helping individuals find their best way through the programme
- encouraging learners to interact with one another to resolve difficulties and carry out project work
- maintaining motivation by encouragement
- keeping learning steps challenging but achievable
- giving examples and personalizing the learning material
- giving instant, personal feedback on performance.

The manager of an e-learning programme thus has to consider:

- how support will be provided within the learning material (see Chapters 9 and 10)
- what support will be provided in addition to the materials.

In this chapter we look at the stages of a typical e-learning programme, at the help learners might need at each stage and we suggest who can provide it. We then focus particularly on the person often contracted to help learners succeed in their programme: the tutor. What skills do tutors need and how, as programme manager, can you find the right people? We look briefly at issues of cost and quality. We also include a section on learner expectations, as what learners expect from an e-learning tutor can sometimes be problematic.

Stages of support

Learners pass through a number of stages when taking a programme. We suggest six:

- before they join the programme
- on joining the programme
- the first few weeks of learning
- during the programme
- at the point of final assessment
- after completion.

These will vary in length, depending on the programme, the learner and the context. At each stage the kind of help learners need is different. We look at each stage in turn and suggest what help learners may need and how you might provide it.

BEFORE JOINING

The help individuals need before joining a programme will depend in particular on how much choice the learner is presented with. At one extreme there is no choice, for example where an employer requires a particular employee to take a specific programme; at the other extreme learners may have to make their own choice from a wide range of options.

Before they join a programme learners may need to know:

- what the programme covers and if it is suitable for them
- why it is worth doing
- how it fits in with other training and development activities
- what prior knowledge or experience they need
- how long the programme will take them.

Help at this stage thus includes clear information about the programme: its outcomes, methods of assessment and duration.

You can provide much of this help directly, for example in a brochure or via an electronic database, such as Learnddirect, or by supplying frequently asked questions and answers. You may also need to provide access to a helpline or other source of additional information, such as a training administrator or learning centre receptionist who could answer further questions. Other possible sources of help are line managers or employees who have previously taken the programme. In some circumstances the person should be chosen because of their capacity to offer an unbiased view based on professional knowledge – a careers adviser, for example.

A quiz or questionnaire can help an individual decide whether a particular programme is likely to interest them; a pre-test can show whether the individual has the necessary knowledge or skill to succeed in the programme (see Chapters 5 and 7 for more on pre-tests).

There may be a number of outcomes to the first stage. The learner may decide that:

- their original goal was unrealistic and they need to revise it
- their original goal would not be met by the programme
- they need to carry out some preparatory work before joining the programme
- they can join the programme straightaway.

The value of the support provided is that it helps individuals clarify the best way forward; in some cases *not* to join a programme can be a positive choice.

CHECKLIST: PRE-JOINING

Will you offer support at the pre-joining stage?
If yes, how will learners access this support?

- Electronically?
- Face-to-face?
- By telephone?
- Via pre-prepared material?
- By an appointment with someone within the organization?
- By contacting an external adviser?
- By a number of means?

How will you resource the support?

ON JOINING THE PROGRAMME

Let's assume that the individual has decided to join the programme. They might then need:

- more detailed information, for example about the programme's structure, equipment and resources needed, a study timetable
- advice on how to join, for example how to pay any fees, completion of a joining form.

Again, information can be provided electronically, with or without the opportunity to interact with a representative of the programme.

This stage also gives you the opportunity to collect information on the learner, including their relevant experience and qualifications and any special circumstances, such as difficulty in accessing equipment or other resources relevant to the programme.

CHECKLIST: INFORMATION ON LEARNERS

What additional information will you provide for learners when they join?
How will this be made available?

- Electronically?
- In printed form?

Will learners be able to contact a support person? If so, who?

- Administrator?
- Tutor? Mentor?

And how?

- Hot line?
- Meeting?

What information will you collect on newly joined learners? How?

THE FIRST FEW WEEKS OF LEARNING

The first few weeks of learning can prove something of a culture shock, especially to individuals who have not studied recently. They may feel overwhelmed, perhaps having just received a substantial learning package. In the early stages learners can spend a great deal of time familiarizing themselves with electronic learning resources. If they are working from home, this may mean they incur online costs. Learners may be thinking they have taken on too much; they may be worried about their ability to cope.

Learners may thus need support: further explanation of the programme, reassurance about the first assessment, help in planning a timetable, advice on how to use online time economically. Early contact with their tutor is usually a good idea, whether this is by telephone, post, e-mail, or face-to-face . Hence in many programmes tutors introduce themselves to their learners right at the start, for example by sending a biography and a photograph together with a welcoming note.

CHECKLIST: SUPPORT FOR LEARNERS EARLY IN THE PROGRAMME

What additional information will you provide learners in the first few weeks of the programme?
How will this be made available?
Will learners be able to contact a support person?

- Who?
- How?
- At what times are they available?

MID-COURSE

At this stage the learner is either making good progress, is falling behind or has dropped out. It is important to keep track of how the learner is doing and to intervene if necessary – preferably before problems occur. Support mid-course may include:

- reminding learners of key dates
- following up any late submission of projects or assessments
- contacting learners who are not taking part in electronic dialogue (such as conferences)
- answering learners' questions.

Early and regular contact can prevent problems occurring. Some help may be automated; other help may be provided by a tutor or administrator. Less formal sources of support can also be used, such as encouraging learners to contact their colleagues or people who have previously taken the programme. Figure 8.2 demonstrates how on online system can provide mid-course performance data.

Learners who wish to withdraw from the programme may need sensitive help. Here a tutor or sympathetic administrator may be key to providing a personal touch.

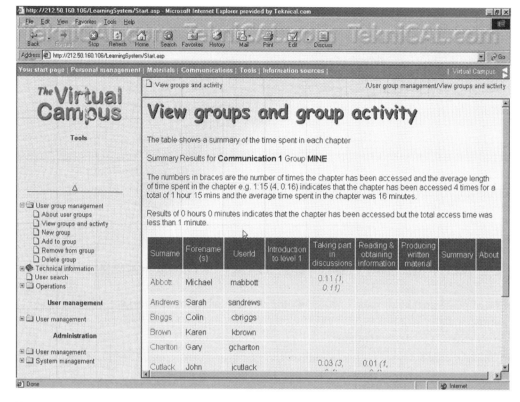

Figure 8.2   A report summarizing learner activity

CHECKLIST: MID-PROGRAMME SUPPORT

How will you keep in contact with learners throughout the programme?
How will you identify learners who are having difficulties?
How will you respond to a learner who wishes to leave the programme?

FINAL ASSESSMENT/LEAVING POINT

The learner may have to submit a final assessment (such as a project), take a practical test of competence or sit a traditional examination. This can trigger a number of concerns, for example nervousness or uncertainty as to what is involved. Help can be provided in the form of:

- advice on preparing for the final assessment
- provision of opportunities to practise or rehearse.

As with the earlier stages, some of this can be pre-prepared in electronic or printed form; or a tutor or other supporter could be accessed (by one or other medium).

CHECKLIST: LEAVING THE PROGRAMME

What signals the end of your programme?
What challenges might the learner face at this stage?
What help might you need to give, in what form and by what means?

AFTER THE PROGRAMME

The learner has now completed the programme and acquired new knowledge, skills or attitudes. They might be wondering what to do next. At this stage they might need:

- to celebrate their success
- to get a profile of their strengths and weaknesses
- to explore other programmes, changes of role or career.

They might thus need advice on further programmes and an opportunity to discuss their future. Some of this can again be managed electronically; in addition, it may be useful to offer a post-programme discussion with a tutor or careers adviser – from within your organization of perhaps from an outside agency. Don't forget the need to celebrate success: some form of award-giving ceremony might be appropriate.

CHECKLIST: POST-PROGRAMME SUPPORT

What support will you provide for learners who have successfully completed their programme?
How will this be provided and who will be involved?
Will you need specialist support from outside your organization?
How will you help learners who have not been successful?
What feedback on their performance will you provide for learners – whether or not they have achieved all the programme outcomes?

Who can help?

As we have seen, support can be provided electronically in a standardized form, for example straightforward information, answers to frequently asked questions and testing with feedback. But there also remains a continuing need for support that is:

- tailored rather than standard
- given by 'a person' rather than by 'the system'.

You will probably be able to call upon a variety of sources of such support, including:

- other learners on the programme
- learners who have previously taken the programme

- colleagues in the workplace
- line managers
- mentors
- trainers
- learning centre or training administrators
- experts/specialists.

One way of categorizing these people is by their geographic proximity to the learners: colleagues in the workplace, for example, will usually be easily accessible face-to-face, but experts may be geographically remote, for example located in a company head office or technical centre.

They can also be categorized by the nature of their existing relationship with the learner. Colleagues at work, for example, are peers: at the same level as the learner. A line manager on the other hand by definition has responsibility for the learner and thus (in a sense) power over them. These differences will affect the help each can provide.

Another way of categorizing the helpers is by the extent to which they have been professionally prepared to give help. Some sources will not have been specifically trained in their support role. The learners' peers and colleagues, for example, may not be qualified as trainers, and they may not be especially expert in the subject matter – though they can nevertheless give very useful general support. But other sources offer 'professional' help of different kinds, as Figure 8.3 shows. The third column is a reminder of the limits of the professionalism of each source.

Professional	Source of expertise	Limits to expertise
Technical specialist	Content or skill the programme is trying to teach	May not be trained at helping people to learn
Learning centre administrator	Knowledge of training packages on different topics; knowledge of resources needed to use the packages	May not be able to advise on applications of the programme in the workplace
Trainer	Skills in facilitating learning	May not have expertise in the technical content of the programme

Figure 8.3   Professional sources of support

The key to designing an effective system is to use each source of support at its point of strength. Each can then complement the other. Figure 8.4 shows the particular type of support each source can offer.

Source of support	Type of support
Other learners	Exchange views on the learning material; help with difficulties; joint working on projects
Colleagues in the workplace	Moral support; access to equipment and so on at work; help with projects
Line managers	Access to workplace equipment/experiences; support with study (for example facilities, time off)
Mentors	Help in relating programme to career aspirations; advice on how to resolve conflicts (at work or at home) triggered by learning; review of progress on personal timetable
Learning centre/training administrators	Information and advice on the programme (and other programmes); access to learning resources and related equipment; technical support (for example updates/trouble-shooting)
Experts/specialists	Resolution of technical questions; advice on latest developments and/or applications within a particular organization
Tutors	See the next section

Figure 8.4   Different kinds of support

The learner will be responsible for taking the initiative for activating some of these sources. As programme manager you will, for example, be unlikely to make support from colleagues a formal part of the support offered – though you may well remind learners of the value of such support and suggest uses they can make of it. It will be your responsibility, though, to plan the more formal support, for example access to administrators or company experts. In these cases, the arrangements for availability need to be agreed with all concerned and explained to learners, for example the opening hours of a helpline and the speed with which e-mail questions will be answered.

CHECKLIST: PERSONAL SUPPORT

Will you offer 'tailored' support to individuals?
If so, who will provide this?
What arrangements will you need to make to ensure this help is available?
What information needs to be given to learners to help them make full use of help (whether this is informal or provided as part of the programme)?

We have discussed a range of people who can help learners. One source is so important that we have given them a section to themselves: tutors–people whose professional expertise lies in helping individuals learn.

The tutor

Years of experience of open and distance learning show that the tutor is often the crucial element in a learner's success – and in whether or not learners have a positive view of their programme. More recent evidence suggests that this is just as true for e-learning.

First, a word about terms. We use 'tutor' throughout to describe the person appointed with a specific expertise in, and responsibility for, helping people to learn. Words familiar in more traditional education and training are misleading: the e-tutor does not 'lecture'; 'teacher' and 'trainer' are also too closely associated with 'stand up and deliver' activity; 'instructor' in the UK at least implies a rather limited and one-way role.

WHAT THE TUTOR DOES

Tutors carry out a range of activities, showing the importance of the role. Not all tutors in all schemes carry out every activity: one of the challenges facing you as manager is to decide which are the most significant activities in your programme. The activities carried out by the tutor will depend on the context. Some tutors are responsible for individuals (working on their own), others for groups (learning together via videoconferencing); some for learners working at home, whom they never see, others whom they might meet in a company's learning centre.

We look at five aspects of the tutor's role, though there are overlaps between them:

- facilitator of learning
- manager
- assessor
- host/hostess
- technical advisor.

The most important role is that of facilitator of learning. Here the tutor acts as a guide or consultant to the learner. This kind of input should have been used at the programme design stage: tutors have a contribution to make to decisions about the structure of the programme, its outcomes, the activities through which learners achieve programme outcomes, and the assessment arrangements. The more they are involved in the design stage the better: it helps them subsequently to support learners with the necessary commitment and first-hand knowledge. In e-learning the facilitator role is sometimes also described as 'chair', 'convenor' or 'moderator'.

The role of facilitator overlaps with that of 'manager'. In this role the tutor maintains the structure and coherence of the programme for the learner. This is particularly important in e-learning: to help learners feel comfortable in an environment which can otherwise seem out of their sight and out of their control.

The tutor might also have to act as manager in a more traditional sense of the word, in representing the provider, for example in implementing any rules for late submission of assessments or clarifying queries relating to payment of programme fees.

The activities of 'assessor' are well-established. Tutors in face-to-face environments frequently carry the responsibility for assessment as well as for teaching and this is also often the case in e-learning. As we have seen from Chapters 5 and 7, assessment is of major importance both to consolidate learning (by giving the learner feedback) and as part of the formal process of accreditation.

The tutor also has a social function. Language rather fails us here: there is no one generally agreed word that summarizes the way tutors create a comfortable and friendly learning environment. We have chosen 'host/hostess', but this is not ideal as it carries connotations of a rather trivial, old-fashioned and formal activity; in fact the role is directly linked to learning.

Finally, the e-learning tutor will usually also have a role in helping learners use the necessary technology. Tutors should not be expected to be technical specialists: software designers and technical experts will carry out that function. But the tutor is in direct contact with learners and thus is in an excellent position to help them understand and use the technology for the purposes of learning.

We summarize in Figure 8.5 some of the activities associated with each facet of the tutor's role.

Role	Activities
Facilitator	Questioning, challenging learners Answering questions Setting tasks Presenting alternative viewpoints Drawing knowledge from the group Summarizing Linking different aspects/components of the programme Linking messages Modelling good online behaviour Reminding learners of programme outcomes and how these are assessed Advising on learning methods Addressing learner expectations (see next section)
Manager	Setting, issuing, updating agendas and timetables Reminding learners of impending deadlines Dealing with requests for late submission of assessments Sharing out tasks and responsibilities amongst the learner group Monitoring electronic contributions Explaining programme regulations
Assessor	Giving learners feedback on their work Helping learners identify areas of performance to develop Providing formal accreditation of learner competence
Host/hostess	Welcoming learners, for example to an e-tutorial Acknowledging individuals and their contributions Helping learners to work with one another Using an appropriate and inclusive tone Replying promptly to learner questions
Technical adviser	Inducting learners into the technical platform Showing good practice in using technology for learning Advising on message management (printing out, deleting, filing, archiving)

Figure 8.5   The role of the tutor

As with the skilled face-to-face tutor, the e-tutor will move easily in and out of these activities. Sometimes they will lead the group, sometimes stand back for others to take the initiative. They will encourage reticent learners to contribute, agree meeting agendas, answer specific questions, coach an individual in difficulty with a particular aspect of the programme. The e-tutor will be aware of the role they are in at any particular time and what they hope to achieve. They will also help learners become more aware of the variety of help tutors can provide. This is important because learners may be unfamiliar with what tutors do in an e-learning programme.

CHECKLIST: THE TUTOR'S ROLE

Which roles will tutors play in your programme?
What activities will they carry out?

Learner expectations

You need to consider the expectations learners will have of your programme. These will be generated by their previous encounters with education and training, probably based on conventional classroom teaching, for e-learning is still relatively new. Learners will have assumptions about what the tutor will or should do, and also about their own behaviour (and that of other learners). Some of these assumptions may not be at all appropriate to the programme you have developed, as Figure 8.6 shows.

Assumption	Feature of the programme
Learning is about memorizing information	The outcomes relate to applying information in the workplace
The tutor will give them the content they need	They have to seek out content for themselves, for example on the Web
It's up to the tutor to get them through	Individuals are responsible for their own learning
They will learn on their own	Learners are often assessed on working in groups
You can't rely on the views of other learners	Other learners can be important sources of information
You learn best in face-to-face classes	Most contact is electronic

Figure 8.6 Mismatches between learner assumptions and programme features

The entries in the right-hand column are all typical features of e-learning. If your learners are likely to come with the expectations on the left-hand side you will need to plan accordingly, for example:

- by making clear your own expectations of what tutors and learners will do
- by helping students acquire the strategies of the independent learner, including managing their time, finding resources, evaluating their own work and withstanding the many distractions that may exist in their home and work environments.

Learners may need to develop confidence in study methods unfamiliar to them, for example:

- using technology as a learning tool
- handling large quantities of information
- communicating with a tutor (and other students) whom they may never see.

The technology used in e-learning may impose particular constraints. Some learners may not be proficient in using a mouse and keyboard; they may lack familiarity with icons and short cuts. They may have difficulty keeping on top of all the information that tends to proliferate in electronic environments – deciding whether to delete, store, print out or reply to particular messages. A face-to-face class takes place in a clearly defined time and space; interactions are instantaneous. In e-learning the time and space can seem limitless and unstructured; the gap between receiving messages and replying to them can be considerable; replies may conflict with one another and a tutor may not be immediately available (as in face-to-face) to clarify or arbitrate.

In e-learning the individual is often left to collect and structure their own information. This contrasts with face-to-face teaching, where the tutor usually tries to present information in a coherent and complete way. It also contrasts with distance learning, where the learner is usually provided with a well-structured core resource.

The learner may also be frustrated because of the time they seem to be spending 'getting nowhere' with unfamiliar or slow technology– and anxious about the costs of being online (for example when they are working from home).

Information overload is an ever-present risk. Electronic resources make it all too easy for tutors to send more and more content and suggest apparently endless sources of further information. Once set free on the Web, learners risk being intimidated by the extent of available material. They thus have to learn the skills of information management, such as:

- keeping a clear focus on their own goals
- working out whether a particular source might be of value (before accessing it)
- weighing up the credibility of information suppliers
- handling effectively the resources they do select.

Communicating electronically also presents challenges. Individuals will be used to communicating face-to-face and also by writing. E-communication is somewhere between the two, so they will need to adapt their existing literacy skills. Otherwise they risk upsetting other people by appearing brusque, rude or thoughtless.

Two particular problems represent two sides of the coin: the dominant individual and the learner who opts out. Some learners dominate by the frequency and tone of their contributions; others (for whatever reason) fail to participate in exchanges. Again, the tutor can play a crucial role in helping individuals avoid these potential problems by encouraging effective e-communication and helping learners develop appropriate skills.

Some strategies tutors can use to handle communication issues are set out in Figure 8.7.

Issue	Action
Learners are uneasy about the lack of face-to-face contact	Show that there are electronic equivalents to face-to-face contact help learners acquire the skills to learn from electronic sources/ electronic means of communication
Learners are bewildered by the variety of sources from which they have to learn and the extent of material available on the Web	Help learners focus on their outcomes, on how these will be assessed, and on developing information-handling skills
Learners are unfamiliar with e-learning	Build independent learning skills into the programme; point out that they are not 'on their own' but have colleagues, a tutor, and so on with whom they can interact
Learners are used to a formal classroom environment	Help learners to plan and manage a study environment in their homes/workplace including developing filing systems and avoiding distractions
Technological problems	Help learners set up and run the software; show good practice in your use of the technology; provide telephone helplines
Lack of familiarity with using technology for the purpose of learning	Model good practice; ask questions/challenge learners in ways that lead them naturally to use the technology
Information overload	Teach information management skills
Unfamiliarity with the 'rules' of e-communication	Induct learners into good 'messaging skills' – the characteristics of good/bad messages; the dangers of dominance/withdrawal

Figure 8.7   Helping learners feel comfortable with e-learning

CHECKLIST: ADDRESSING LEARNER EXPECTATIONS

What expectations will learners bring to your programme?
Are these likely to conflict with your programme design?
What action will you take to address learner expectations?
What will the role of the tutor be in addressing learner expectations?

Skills tutors need

Thus the role of the tutor can make all the difference to an individual on an e-learning programme. In many ways the role is similar to that played by a tutor in a well-run conventional class; in other ways it differs. First, the similarities: Figure 8.8 shows the core skills which underlie both e-tutoring and tutoring in conventional circumstances.

Core skill	Examples
Social skills	Welcoming learners; showing sensitivity to individual needs; showing awareness of, and if necessary addressing, learner expectations
Listening	'Reading between the lines': interpreting what is behind what the learner says or (in e-learning) writes
Questioning	Keeping the learner active by asking questions; using different types of question for different purposes
Giving feedback	Giving learners adequate information on their performance and helping them decide what action to take
Leading and taking part in discussion	Stimulating contributions; extending learners' thinking; encouraging quieter learners to contribute; knowing when to hold back and let others take the lead
Assessing	Fairness; care and thoroughness; promptness; accuracy
Efficiency	Maintaining learner records; providing timely information to programme managers and learners
Technical competence	Familiarity with the technology and its uses for learning; acting as a role model in using technology
Understanding of learning	Helping students develop learning skills such as communicating electronically, managing time, working with others, carrying out projects
Improving own performance	Collecting feedback from learners and using this to develop their practice as an e-learning tutor

Figure 8.8   Core tutoring skills

Though these skills are common, they have to be expressed differently in e-learning. Some tutors find it difficult to make the transition from face-to-face to distant contact, missing the 'buzz' of learners interacting in a group where each is physically present to the other. They may also miss the opportunities for performance which traditional training makes possible; in e-learning the tutor has little chance to display that kind of expertise. In e-learning tutors will also often be members of the team rather than solo performers.

Tutors may also feel deprived of the forms of control with which they are familiar. In a conventional class or training session the tutor is the clear and acknowledged source of power: they determine what goes on and their wishes are (usually) carried out by learners. In e-learning, power is much less tangible; it is more dispersed, and learners can more easily take the initiative. Linked to this is the greater informality of e-learning; this too can be perceived as a threat by more traditional teachers.

Some tutors will also be uncomfortable having to support a curriculum that has at least partly been shaped by other people. Face-to-face trainers are usually responsible for their own selection and organization of content; in e-learning this selection will probably have been made by others, at the design stage. Thus e-tutors have to support learning outcomes, assessment and learner activities that they have not themselves planned. In e-learning the tutor is much less important as a source of knowledge and expertise than in traditional training. Their expertise lies rather in supporting individual students and facilitating learning by electronic means.

Finally, some traditional teachers secretly like their students to be at least a little dependent on them. This should no longer be an option in e-learning, where the learner needs to grow as quickly as possible into making their own choices and decisions. E-tutors need to be committed to working to help learners become increasingly independent.

Managing tutors

SELECTING TUTORS

Your specification for tutors is likely to include the following attributes:

- an understanding of learning skills and especially of those needed in an electronic environment
- an easy and pleasant manner which they can communicate across a distance
- information management
- an interest in individuals and in helping them to achieve their objectives
- a preparedness to help learners grow in independence
- the ability to initiate and sustain dialogue
- the ability to give good feedback
- good administration
- the capacity to reflect on, and improve, their own performance.

You will be also be looking for:

- good team players
- who are familiar with using technology in a learning context

- and who are confident that technology can replace more traditional means of contact between tutors and learners
- and are prepared to work with a curriculum they may not themselves have designed.

CHECKLIST: CHOOSING A TUTOR

What skills will your tutors need?
Where will you find your tutors:

- within the organization?
- outside (for example via a college, on freelance contracts)?

A TUTOR JOB DESCRIPTION

You will need to translate your broad tutor brief into a job description. This will include a list of activities the tutor will be expected to carry out, as in the example below.

The tutor will be expected to:

- prepare and post a biography of themselves, with a photograph
- send an e-mail to each new learner within 36 hours of their enrolment
- acknowledge receipt of assessments within 48 hours
- provide feedback on assessments within five days, following the guidance notes on feedback
- assess learner performance using assessment criteria and accompanying notes
- be available for learner helpline access at agreed times (minimum two hours per week)
- maintain up-to-date records of learner progress
- provide input to conferences/noticeboards as appropriate
- convene online tutorials in accordance with the programme timetable
- monitor learner contributions to activities and intervene as necessary
- monitor on- and off-line conferences and intervene as necessary, for example by closing down 'dead' conferences.

The detail of your job description will depend upon your programme. In some schemes tutors will need to convene face-to-face classes as well as make electronic contact; if the tutor is available by phone then this may be only at set times or on a more open-ended basis. You will note that the above extract from a job description begins to set standards for the work of the tutor. This enables you to monitor the quality of your tutorial provision (see Chapter 2).

CHECKLIST: THE JOB DESCRIPTION

What will be the main headings of the job description for your tutors?

INDUCTING, TRAINING AND SUPPORTING TUTORS

By now you will have a clear idea of the role tutors will be playing in your programme and of the skills they will need to play this role. You should also have begun to operationalize these into activities and standards. You are thus in a position to decide what kind of induction tutors will need for your programme. You might also need to develop a training programme. Areas you might cover in induction and training are:

- the technological platform
- the desktop (icons and so on)
- how to carry out various procedures (for example send messages)
- protocols for good online behaviour
- running synchronous learning events
- moderating conferences (online/off-line)
- handling difficult situations (for example overconfident or passive learners).

Some of these areas require briefing rather than training, for example the ways in which functions are handled within a particular platform. Others involve more complex behaviours, such as handling 'difficult' learners. Some require pedagogic knowledge, for example assessing learning styles and deciding what to do in the light of the findings. A training and development programme will usually be needed to cover these more complex activities.

You will also need to provide briefing materials to tutors, to reinforce the more formal documentation, such as job descriptions and contracts. This is particularly important if they are involved in assessment (see Chapter 7). These tutor briefing materials should be developed alongside the learner materials, to ensure integration.

CASE STUDY: A TRAINING PROGRAMME FOR TUTORS

We were responsible for devising a training programme for tutors in Hungary. Tutors worked through an open learning package to prepare for a one-day workshop, which was followed by further self-study and then an assessment. The pre-work included three assignments: assessing (and giving feedback on) learners' work, planning a tutorial and writing a tutor biography. The workshop included peer analysis of the pre-work, practice in using the telephone and electronic methods of communicating, and giving feedback. After the workshop the participants explored record-keeping and the role of the tutor in helping learners organize their work. Finally, the tutors were assessed on a written examination and on a log of competence.

COSTS AND QUALITY

As manager you will be keen to secure a good quality learner support system for a reasonable cost. As part of this, you should apply the principle of using the most skilled (and usually the most expensive) person – the tutor – for the most complex tasks. The less complex tasks can be allocated to less sophisticated sources of support. An administrator in a learning resource centre will, for example, usually be paid less than a trainer and will also be well able to handle many routine learner queries. It would not be cost-efficient to use a tutor for this. Mentors, line managers and learners' colleagues will generally be able to offer their support through goodwill or as part of their existing role.

It is also cost-efficient to automate as many processes as possible; technology can, for example, be used to respond to frequently asked questions. Consider the way in which modern banking has removed the need for face-to-face contact with counter staff and bank managers. As well as being in itself an important educational goal, helping learners to become less dependent also reduces support costs: they sort out many problems for themselves.

If you are providing a tutor, or other professional source of support, you should ensure the role is clearly defined. Tutors will then know exactly what is expected of them, and learners will know what they are entitled to. You need particularly to ensure that learners understand what demands they can make, for what purposes, and how they can access various kinds of help.

Other ways of managing the costs of learner support are:

- minimizing face-to-face contacts
- briefing and training tutors (and learners) electronically
- creating economies of scale (for example an allocation of learners to tutors that achieves critical mass)
- careful initial programme design.

Another important task is to monitor tutors and check the quality of the support they offer. Like learners, tutors also need (and usually welcome) feedback on their performance:

- on the quality of their feedback on assessments
- on the accuracy of their grading
- on the quality of the information they provide
- on their skill at running online sessions.

Encourage interaction between tutors, for example via a conference site. This helps spread good practice.

SUMMARY

- How can you automate aspects of the support you offer learners?
- Have you planned full use of less expensive sources of support?
- Are you using the tutor for tasks that require professional expertise?
- Are you encouraging learners to become more self-reliant?
- Have you made clear the support that will be offered, how and where it will be offered and how learners can access it?
- How will you monitor the performance of your support services?
- How will you encourage the spread of good tutoring practice?
- What arrangements will you make for the briefing and training of tutors?

9 Managing Materials Selection and Adaptation

THIS CHAPTER WILL HELP YOU:

- decide what type of learning package you need
- search for suitable existing materials
- evaluate the materials you find
- decide what (if any) adaptations you need to make
- prepare a study guide (if appropriate)
- plan the stages of producing any additional material.

Learning materials provide the core content in most e-learning schemes. They make it possible for the learner to study without the constant presence of a tutor or trainer. You can consider various alternative sources of these materials, as shown below.

Using materials already developed   Developing your own materials

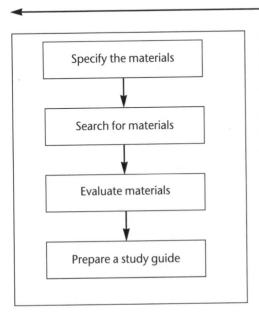

On the left are materials that have already been developed; in electronic form, these are sometimes known as 'learning objects'. At the other extreme is preparing your own entirely new materials/learning objects. But there are many positions in between, all of which involve either adaptation of what already exists (tending towards the left-hand side) or the production of new materials (tending towards the right-hand side). We begin this chapter with an examination of options towards the left, because here you are most likely to:

- save time
- save expense
- minimize stress.

Figure 9.1 A sequence for selecting and adapting learning materials

Figure 9.1 sets out a sequence for selecting and adapting learning materials.

Specifying the materials you want

Based on your reading of the earlier chapters you should have a reasonably clear idea of the kind of learning package you need, that is the functions you want the material to perform, given your target learner group and what they have to learn. Here, for example, is a possible list of functions for the material:

- arouse the learner's interest
- state clear outcomes (and these are the outcomes you want)
- structure the content for ease of learning
- give opportunities for learners to practise
- give feedback on the practice
- explain difficult ideas or processes
- set up a dialogue with the learner.

Once you have decided which functions are important to you, you then know what features to look for in the learning material. Some examples of features are shown in Figure 9.2.

All the time you are concentrating on your learners: what will help them learn? You will also need to be aware of the other points made in Chapters 1 and 2, such as the role of any additional support to be provided (for example by a tutor or mentor) and the constraints within which you have to work (for example your budget).

Function	Sample features
Arouse the learner's interest	Good lay out and illustrations; use of examples and case studies
State clear outcomes	What the learner should achieve is set out in straightforward, understandable language
Structure the content for ease of learning	Topics are grouped in convenient 'chunks' for learning; clear introductions and summaries
Give opportunities for learners to practise	Activities, exercises, questions, projects
Give feedback on the practice	Answers to questions and exercises; comments on activities; checklists to guide work on projects
Explain difficult ideas or processes	Clear, straightforward language; use of examples and case studies
Set up a dialogue with the learner	Friendly style; use of questions; incorporate online communication

Figure 9.2   Functions and features of learning material

Searching for materials

You are now in a position to look for a suitable package. You can look in a number of places: within your own organization (almost too obvious?) and sources that may be more remote. Searching on the Web enables you to investigate not only national but also international sources. As well as publishers, you might search organizations similar to your own, colleges, training providers and professional networks.

The following checklist gives some ideas on how you might set about finding learning materials.

CHECKLIST: FINDING MATERIALS

Search the Web.
Ask a librarian/someone with search skills to help.
Publicize your needs within relevant networks.
Attend relevant conferences/seminars.
Join relevant user groups.
Search directories.
Look widely, for example not confining yourself to material in any one medium.

Evaluating the material

You may have uncovered a number of different resources/types of resource, for example:

- materials designed for use by learners in your target group
- structured learning material but not designed specifically for use in e-learning
- structured learning material but not designed specifically for your learner group
- education or training material strong on content but not easy to learn from
- informational material not designed for learning (for example technical data, promotional material)
- lists of relevant websites, books and other resources.

Your next task is to evaluate this material. You know from your specification what features you are looking for. From this you can draw up a checklist to guide your evaluation. Here is a sample checklist; yours may well include different items, relevant to the particular requirements of your programme.

CHECKLIST: EVALUATING MATERIALS

Are learning outcomes specified? Do they match your requirements?
Is the right content covered? Are there any gaps? Is some content irrelevant?
Is the content up to date?
Is the style appropriate for the target learners (for example clear vocabulary, short sentences and paragraphs)?

Are there any special technical requirements?

Is the content divided into suitable 'chunks' (for example maximum one hour's learning time)? Are these linked coherently together (for example via a modular structure)?

Can learners start at different points according to their needs? Are flexible routes through the programme possible?

Is the content structured for ease of use by learners (for example by headings, sub-headings, a contents page, an index, a glossary of key terms)?

Does the material look attractive (for example layout, use of illustrations)?

Is the medium of presentation appropriate?

Is the material affordable?

Are there opportunities for the learner to practise (for example questions, activities, ideas for work-based projects)?

Is sufficient feedback provided for learners?

Does the material lead to accreditation for those learners who want this?

Will the material remain available (for example if online, will it continue to be maintained and supported; if a book, will it stay in print/are there likely to be new editions)?

It is a good idea to involve other people in the evaluation. Figure 9.3 shows examples of whom you might involve, and the perspective they might bring to evaluating the material.

Group	Perspective
Colleagues	Similar to your own; useful check
Subject specialists	Their expertise means you can check the accuracy and currency of content
Sponsors (for example line managers)	The view of a customer
Tutors	They may subsequently have to support learners using the material
Sample learners	Main users of the material

Figure 9.3   Evaluation of learning material

Deciding what changes to make

Your evaluation may lead to one of the following decisions:

- reject the material as unsuitable
- approve the material as fully meeting your requirements
- use the material provided it is modified or supplemented.

If the decision is to reject then you need proceed no further with that package. On the other hand, rarely is any resource fully suitable as it stands: it will be unlikely to cover exactly the content you need in a way that matches perfectly the needs of your learner group. So the final option – modification – is the most likely.

Your evaluation will probably have left you with a list of changes you need to make, as in the example given in Figure 9.4.

Aspect of the material	Action needed to make the material suitable
Content	Update certain sections Advise learners to ignore certain sections Link content to learners' contexts (for example via case studies) Fill some gaps, including references to other resources Expand on topics learners find difficult (for example via worked examples) Add a glossary of key terms
Structure	Add learning outcomes to guide users Advise learners on the order in which to study topics Advise users on how to break up the content into study sessions
Practice and feedback	Add exercises/questions (with answers/feedback) Prepare assessment material Add frequently asked questions (with answers)
Other	Add a guide to the programme Add advice on how to study Add a Help facility Provide tutor briefing

Figure 9.4   Sample modifications to an existing package

Preparing a study guide

One way to make such changes is to prepare a study guide. This is simply an additional resource you prepare to accompany the learning material you have identified. Preparing a study guide has a number of advantages, for example:

- you can use existing materials and this avoids the time, expense and trouble of preparing your own
- you don't have to change the resources themselves (unless you wish to) – the study guide is additional to them
- learners are helped to make full use of the materials you have identified.

Furthermore, involving tutors (and others in your programme) in preparing the study guide will increase their sense of ownership of the result: they are more likely to feel it is 'their' programme, rather than just bought-in from outside.

One way of viewing the study guide is that it provides the equivalent of what good teachers or trainers do in a well-run traditional class; for example:

- using a direct, friendly style
- presenting material in an order that makes sense for learning
- explaining points that learners always find difficult
- giving examples that help learners see the relevance of a point
- explaining why the content is important to learn
- answering frequently asked questions
- defining key terms
- steering learners between various resources, providing a thread for them to follow, as in the example given in Figure 9.5)

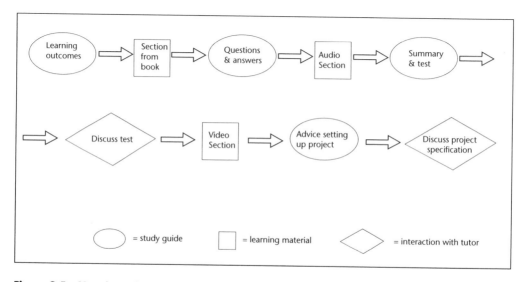

Figure 9.5   Use of a study guide with a programme

Your own tutoring or training staff will probably be very skilled at these things and used to incorporating them, for example in handouts or Powerpoint presentations. Thus, with careful briefing, they should be able to help with the preparation of the study guide, whether as authors or by providing comments.

You will need to produce a specification for the study guide, covering not only its contents but also its appearance. You will want to make it attractive and easy to use.

Planning production of the study guide

You will then need to schedule the remaining work, as in the checklist below.

CHECKLIST: STAGES IN THE PRODUCTION OF A STUDY GUIDE

Decide what changes are to be made
Identify/commission an author
Get comments on the first draft (for example from colleagues, tutors, sample learners)
Manage the revision of the guide
Produce a pilot version of the guide
Decide what changes are to be made after piloting
Produce the final version
Monitor use of the guide and adapt it as necessary

The time all this will take will depend on the extent of your study guide.

A NOTE ON COPYRIGHT

One of the benefits of preparing a study guide is that you will avoid the difficulty of changing the original package. To do this would require negotiations with the publisher, either to make the changes or to allow you to make them.

In preparing the study guide you have to observe current copyright legislation. If you wish to reproduce material from other copyright sources you will have to ask permission. To do this you need to provide full details of the source:

- author
- publication date
- precise description of the extract you want to use
- what you plan to do with the material (for example who will use it and for what purposes)
- how the material will be distributed (for example freely available online, available only to registered learners)
- relevant financial arrangements (for example whether learners will pay).

These details will enable the copyright holder to decide whether or not to charge you, and how much. You need to contact the copyright holder early, as clearance can take several weeks.

SUMMARY
• •

- To maximize time, resources and quality, whenever possible you should use existing materials, adapted as necessary.
- Define the kind of learning package you need, based on your analysis of programme content and on your learner group.
- Search for materials that may meet your specification.
- Evaluate the materials you find, using your specification.
- If the materials are basically suitable, decide what changes/additions need to be made.

10 Developing and Acccessing Learning Materials

THIS CHAPTER WILL HELP YOU:

- select and use media in delivering learning programmes
- choose development software for e-learning
- choose delivery software for e-learning
- use learning portals and learning management systems
- schedule and resource the in-house development of e-learning
- decide whether and how to use a learning centre in delivering your programme.

This chapter is divided into four main parts:

- media available for use in e-learning, their advantages and disadvantages
- criteria for selecting media
- platforms available for developing your own learning material and for delivering it
- the stages involved in developing materials and how to schedule these
- the use of learning centres as a means by which participants can access your programme and get support as they study.

Media selection

A range of media is available to the training manager. These need not (and often should not) be restricted to electronic media. Some options, together with their potential applications, are set out in Figure 10.1.

MEDIA PREFERENCES

A research project published in April 2001 reported on the use of these media by training managers and other staff throughout a wide range of British companies (George and Cooper 2001). The researchers contacted over 1600 companies throughout the UK with a spectrum of size that reflected the national situation. Some of the findings as indicated in Figure 10.2 may be surprising.

Medium	Uses
Textbooks	Present large quantities of factual material Readily available for reference Portable Very occasionally a textbook forms the core of a 'wraparound' study guide that includes activities, questions and feedback (see Chapter 9)
Open learning texts	As for textbooks, also ... Deliver interactive lessons on discrete concepts and skills Modular design to enable access at different points Learner-centred style and approach
Videos	Lecturing Demonstrate individual physical skills (for example use of hand tools) Demonstrate interactive skills (for example negotiating) Case studies Motivation and scene-setting Illustrate normally inaccessible processes or locations (for example chemical processes)
Audio tapes	Lecturing Guiding learners through tasks Case studies Language learning Motivation
Computer-based training (CBT) on CD-ROM	As for open learning texts, also ... Can present randomly chosen examples from a large data bank Can simulate processes and procedures particularly IT-related Can include time controls Caters for learners at different levels and with different styles Administers large-scale assessments Provides information about learner's progress
CBT on intranet (accessible via the company's local or wide area network)	As for CBT, also ... Provides both group and individual learning
CBT on Internet (accessed via the World Wide Web)	As above for CBT on intranet, also ... Can be used to access other resources throughout the WWW

Figure 10.1   Media and their uses

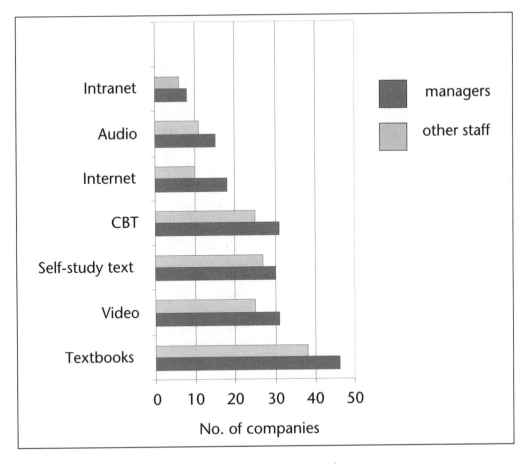

Figure 10.2   Proportion of companies using various training tools

As the authors commented 'The use of on-line learning is still low even amongst the most proactive companies.' The three most popular (that is, used) training tools for both managers and other staff are:

- textbooks
- video tapes
- paper-based materials (e.g. self-study text)

The researchers also explored the extent to which different methods were deemed to meet learners' objectives (Table 10.1). The difference in the judgements of the different media by managers and other staff is remarkable, with other staff consistently rating their satisfaction as significantly lower than managers. The findings suggest that careful thought may be required by those intending to produce a learning package that is distributed in the same format to staff at various levels.

Table 10.1   Percentage of staff for whom training fully met their needs

Materials	Managers	Other staff
Textbooks	87	42
Self study texts	86	77
Videos	79	50
Audio tapes	90	52
CBT	70	53
Intranet	50	—
Internet	100	64

Source: After George and Cooper 2001

ADVANTAGES AND DISADVANTAGES OF THE E-LEARNING OPTION

George and Cooper investigated uses of e-learning (they use the term 'ICT-based learning') in depth. The companies responding to the survey cited various advantages and disadvantages of the method. The most frequently mentioned are listed in order in Figure 10.3. Companies who are already using e-learning tend to emphasize the advantages. Those who have yet to use technology-based methods emphasize the disadvantages.

Advantages	Disadvantages
Flexibility	Learners lack supervision
Fits needs of individuals	Learner isolation
Speed of access	Difficulty of monitoring progress
Cost-effective	Difficulty of selecting materials
Allows people to work at their own pace	It's not as effective as traditional methods
Does not disrupt normal work	Not on-the-job
Self-monitoring	Lack of tuition
Ability to customize training to own needs	
Access to a broader range of subjects	
People enjoy it	
A lot of people can use one package	

Figure 10.3   Advantages and disadvantages of e-learning

The intending e-learning manager should be alert to the items listed in the disadvantages column. E-learning practitioners tend to take it for granted that, by now, the effectiveness of the method is no longer an issue. There is a mass of research evidence that this and other methods of distance learning are as effective as traditional methods of teaching and learning.

But negative views remain prevalent and hard to break down, particularly in organizations where there is little experience in distance learning or limited use of information technology. Given this, we re-emphasize the point made in Chapter 3: you will need to win the backing of top management before the scheme is launched and thereafter to prepare a strategy to encourage both learners and their managers (and tutors) to try the e-learning option.

Criteria for selecting media

We pointed out in Chapter 6 that when the specification is produced, the presentation method to adopt for each module should also be considered. In deciding the media to use, course managers and designers need to bear in mind three sets of considerations:

- suitability to the learning outcomes
- acceptability to learners
- feasibility.

THE LEARNING OUTCOMES FOR THE PROGRAMME

The chosen delivery method must be the most suitable for helping the learners to achieve their own and the organization's objectives. A well-expressed learning outcome will satisfy two key criteria for media selection: practice and fidelity.

Practice

Each module should help learners develop the capability described in the learning outcomes for the programme. For some, skills practice on the real thing may be difficult for such reasons as expense, security, availability of equipment and so on. The training of pilots or surgeons are examples. In these circumstances the programme may use simulators, audio-visual substitutes or computer terminals.

Very often an e-learning programme for learning skills and procedures will comprise a hybrid: concept learning in electronic form and a set of practice items in a printed booklet or binder.

CASE STUDY: TRAINING HOSPITAL ADMINISTRATIVE STAFF

A programme has been produced for training administrative staff in hospitals who assign codes to diseases. The interactive electronic learning sequences explaining and illustrating the coding system include practice with a range of examples of diseases. The questions are of the type 'What code would you assign to a patient who breaks their left wrist falling down stairs?' At the end of the module the learner is tested with much more detailed cases put into context. They consist of passages of continuous text simulating a doctor's notes and may contain 100–200 words. These exercises are more suitable – and realistic - in text form.

Fidelity/transferability

In e-learning the designer often has to find a way of transferring learning from the screen to performance in the working environment. You are more likely to meet this challenge if the learning situation resembles the job as closely as possible. For example where the learning concerns computer-related procedures it is clearly desirable to develop a simulation (or emulation) of the application to be learned. The training modules will then be windowed over that simulation.

Ideally a learning programme on letter writing would at some stage require the learner to write several letters on given topics. Those letters would need to be assessed by a tutor. An e-learning package on written communications – and there are many – cannot be said to be complete without this feature.

An exception to this rule of fidelity occurs when resemblance to real life may actually be undesirable – at least in the early stages of learning. Using real correspondence in a course on dealing with customer letters of complaint would be such a case.

LEARNER ACCEPTABILITY

Earlier in this chapter we quoted research evidence of learners' preferences for different media, noting the surprising nature of some of these. Throughout this book we have tried to stress the central place of the learner in the development process, so learners' views of media need to be considered. Learners like to feel that the package has been developed with their needs in mind rather than according to the preferences of learning designers or accountants.

Many designers and sponsors think that the more advanced the technology the better the learning system. Some learners are, indeed, attracted by high technology presentations, though there is evidence that learners soon become bored with any one technology, particularly if it seems to be used for trivial purposes. Participants generally like to get on and learn something: they are not particularly bothered about the medium as long as it helps them to do this.

In selecting the form in which to present the learning, developers and sponsors should note the following:

- learners are alienated by old, unattractive and deficient course materials
- learners do not like having to share a package
- learners like to get to the point
- learners are not impressed by gimmicks
- learners who are not computer literate may be distracted from the content of the material by the technology.

FEASIBILITY

Your e-learning scheme must be achievable. You thus need to be able to afford the media in terms of both up-front development and running costs.

These are common problems:

- trying to incorporate sound or video within Web-delivered material
- designing the programme for delivery via different browsers
- underestimating the time it will take to complete the project
- linking the programme into the learning management system
- providing support: tutorial support may be an element of your strategy for the programme but being able to provide it reliably – even by e-mail only – is not always easy.

CASE STUDY: E-LEARNING IN A BIOTECHNOLOGY COMPANY

A biotechnology company has developed a series of e-learning modules in Applied Microbiology aimed at technical employees. The aim is 'to improve knowledge of areas relevant to current role and future career'. The training is available online and although the employees use this facility the textbook is preferred because it provides the level of detail required by someone that has already completed a bioscience degree. They feel that less detail is available on the website and it is not easy to navigate and draw information from.

(cited by George and Cooper 2001)

Several of the above criteria are relevant to the case study:

- The objectives are rather vague and thus do not give a strong lead on media selection.
- The emphasis on knowledge rather than skills limits opportunities to provide learner activities and practice.
- The learner group has a strong sense of professional identity and an attachment to previous learning methods that has not been taken into account; this lessens their motivation to use the online approach.

Generally the case study shows an unimaginative use of the online facility, which duplicates what already exists more conveniently in another medium.

Platforms for e-learning development and delivery

So far we have discussed e-learning using existing materials but of course many organizations will be planning to produce their own learning programmes. Courseware production involves two separate but complementary stages: the design of a learning sequence and conversion to electronic format. The former is carried out by someone with pedagogical expertise known as an instructional designer, or simply by the author; the latter is undertaken by a programmer. In this section we look at the decisions that need to be taken about the software that the programmer will use to ensure that lessons are delivered effectively to learners as the author intended.

AUTHORING AND DEVELOPMENT SOFTWARE

Until recently e-learning was characterized by multimedia computer-based training (CBT) delivered on CD-ROM. Users bought in materials off-the-shelf, commissioned them from an external supplier or developed their own. In a business context these packages tended to be stand-alone, self-contained products designed for individual study with little, if any, human support deemed necessary, even if it were feasible or available.

For the production of such packages most corporate developers of CBT use either a programming language, such as C++ or Visual Basic, or one of the so-called authoring systems. Of the latter the most popular in the UK are Macromedia's Authorware and Tool-Book, now distributed by Click2learn. Both these products include special features that speed up the development of CBT packages as compared with a conventional programming language.

The DfES (formerly the DfEE) publication *Technology Based Training and Online Learning* (Dean 2001) describes the essential components of an authoring system. They are:

- facilities that allow developers who may not be computer experts to enter the training content onto screens in an attractive way
- support for linking screens together into modules
- support for a range of question types so that the course designers can choose the most appropriate for a particular situation and provide variety for the learner
- response analysis that takes the learner's answer to questions and provides feedback and branches according to the learner's responses.

There will continue to be a need for this type of material – however it may be delivered – for a wide variety of business applications.

The use of the Internet to deliver learning and the rapid growth of learning management systems have made the e-learning manager's choice of development software far more complex. Both ToolBook and Authorware are examples of CBT authoring systems that have been enhanced so as to be capable of producing multimedia learning for distribution over the Internet. Another option for the intending developer is to use a browser-based language such as HTML (Hypertext Mark-up Language) or Java. These are purpose-designed software systems for generating Web pages and can be programmed to deliver interactive learning for Web delivery of the kind that was previously delivered via CD-ROM.

COMPUTER CONFERENCING AND MESSAGING

Computer conferencing systems and e-mail are used as the basis of the virtual classroom model of e-learning. Computer conferencing enables people to hold a discussion by communicating through a computer network. Each participant has a mailbox to which messages are sent by the other participants from their terminals.

Computer conferencing is the basis of the e-learning model that predominates in further and higher education. Learners in distant locations undertake individual and collaborative activities, receiving feedback from a tutor and other learners. Most learning management systems include a conferencing facility. Many of the effects of conferencing can be equally well achieved by the humble e-mail.

Virtual learning environments (VLE)

There are at least two uses of the term virtual learning environment. Within further and higher education the term means a learning system in which the central feature is a dialogue between the learner and their tutor/s and between them and their peers. This form of the VLE operates by using a web browser to access HTML pages on the server.

The server is capable of:

- creating and displaying dynamic HTML pages
- allowing messages to be posted to conferences or a web noticeboard
- carrying out online assessment
- maintaining a database of information on users, learning materials and course structure.

Examples of VLEs are WebCT and Blackboard (see <http://www.webct.com>; <http://www.blackboard.com>).

There are two users of a VLE, learners and tutors. Both groups will have similar access to the learning materials and related facilities. Additionally tutors will usually have the ability to create new materials, set up conferences and track learner progress.

The basic features of a VLE are shown in Figure 10.4. This functionality requires a learning management system to operate (see Chapter 12). To add to the confusion some practitioners, including vendors, treat the two terms as synonymous.

The other definition of a virtual learning environment is a simulation of a workplace situation. This is the definition more common in the corporate context. For example at Quaker Oats students spend 16 hours 'going to work in the company'. They 'walk' through the building, attend meetings, read reports, receive e-mails, answer the phone and use a computer to query a database. They then write a report recommending a specific course of action.

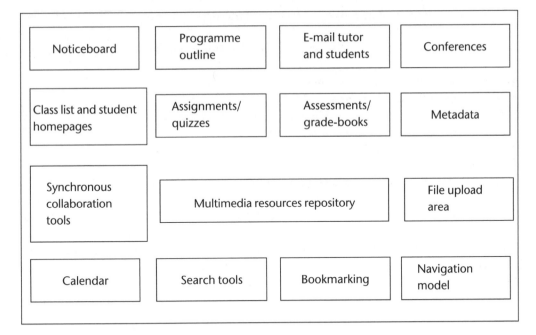

Noticeboard	Programme outline	E-mail tutor and students	Conferences
Class list and student homepages	Assignments/ quizzes	Assessments/ grade-books	Metadata
Synchronous collaboration tools	Multimedia resources repository		File upload area
Calendar	Search tools	Bookmarking	Navigation model

Figure 10.4   Schematic of a prototypical VLE

DEFINING YOUR NEED

Figure 10.5 lists various types of e-learning development systems and gives examples of some of the – mainly proprietary – products that may be used for each type.

Option	Example
Programming languages	C++, Visual Basic
CBT authoring systems	Authorware, ToolBook
Internet coding software	HTML, Java, Flash
Learning management systems / VLEs	Skill Vantage Manager, Teknical, WebCT
Conferencing systems	First Class
Messaging	E-mail

Figure 10.5   E-learning development software

Before selecting development software you will need to answer the following questions:

- Do you need an on-going, full scale corporate learning and knowledge management system?
- Will all the learning take place online?
- How important is tutor involvement?
- How important is it that learners should collaborate over their learning?
- What technical support is available in-house?
- What management facilities will be needed?
- Do you want to run off-the-shelf courseware only?
- If not will you be developing materials in-house?

The answers to these questions will greatly depend on the circumstances of the organization. A learning management system would probably be inappropriate for a smaller company lacking a computer network; a company that needs to do a lot of repetitive IT training may be able to do this using off-the-shelf packages but it may need to keep detailed records of all training undertaken. We shall illustrate the possibilities by reviewing three hypothetical cases. At this stage we shall just pose the problems. Later we shall look at possible solutions.

CASE STUDY A: MOTOR CAR DEALERSHIP

A motor car dealership has 150 employees at four locations in the Midlands. They have several kinds of training need:

a) Parts sales staff need training in customer care.

b) Office staff need training in IT procedures.

c) Car salespeople need to update themselves regularly on new models and financial developments.

Each location has a number of PCs and access to the manufacturer's intranet.

CASE STUDY B: GOVERNMENT DEPARTMENT

A government department has staff at seven locations around the country. Almost all have access to PCs on a network. As part of their IIP scheme there is an appraisal system that identifies training needs on an on-going basis.

Learning centres in each location have a wide range of off-the-shelf materials in print and audio-visual format and on CD-ROM. The department also produces regular print-based distance learning texts for wide distribution to most operational staff and to middle managers on topics such as written communication and time management. The department needs to make the appraisal system and training solutions as accessible as possible.

CASE STUDY C: MEDICAL EQUIPMENT MANUFACTURER

A manufacturer of specialist medical equipment is beginning to distribute nationally an electronic device for use by nurses in GP surgeries for testing for a particular patient condition. Test results are fed back to a central computer via the Internet. All GPs using the device must be online to the Web. The company needs to develop training for all end users in the use of the apparatus.

LEARNING, KNOWLEDGE MANAGEMENT AND PERFORMANCE SUPPORT

Before we consider these cases we shall review some of the technical developments of the recent past and the e-learning tools that are likely to affect the decisions taken in each of the three organizations.

The current position is well summed up by the following quotation:

> E-learning continues to grow past traditional boundaries to encompass all the ways technology can be used to help people learn. That means we're not just talking about on-line courses but also virtual collaboration, knowledge management and other types of data sharing, performance support and job aids. The bottom line is that e-learning in all its various forms gives people immediate access to an abundance of information and knowledge to help them do their jobs better, faster and more effectively.
>
> (Shorrock 2001: 56)

The idea of electronic performance support systems (EPSS) actually predates online learning. An EPSS is a desktop system that integrates learning (for example the explanation of procedures and concepts on request) with basic information (go example contact data for individuals), examples (such as a completed invoice) and guidance (for example the steps of a particular procedure). The suggestion that employees would benefit by having such a system may seem obvious now but since the concept first evolved in the mid-1980s remarkably few organizations have taken it up.

THE LEARNING PORTAL

Before the arrival of the Internet an EPSS would have been hosted on the mainframe computer of larger organizations and accessed from individual users' terminals. Nowadays some larger organizations that have web-based systems provide e-learning and other forms of performance support via what is known as a learning portal. In effect a learning portal is a special kind of website that provides not only e-learning programmes but a range of other support, guidance and information. One expert defines a learning portal as 'a concept rather than a specific product. In essence it is an access point to a set of services via a browser' (Wilson 2000:28).

A learning portal is likely to include:

- a learning management system
  - to manage access to learning programmes and to record student usage and achievement

- development software
  - to create content
- collaborative tools such as a conferencing system
  - to support discussion forums
- student profiling
  - to map skills to job requirements
- links to specific resources.

External portals are accessible to many organizations whereas an internal portal accesses an environment specific to a single organization. This will be delivered on a corporate intranet. The internal portal will make available some or all of the following facilities:

- the corporate university
- internal courses
- discussion forums
- corporate news updates
- links to external training (public courses on the Web).

THE LEARNING MANAGEMENT SYSTEM

These are the most commonly recurring features of learning management systems:

- registering students on to programmes
- processing payments for fees, materials
- providing access to courseware (from different sources)
- tracking learner usage and progress (for example who answered what questions, time taken to complete the course)
- administering tests
- analysing test results
- linking to the WWW
- courseware development templates.

Some organizations design their own learning management systems but the great majority buy one of the many proprietary products on the market. A recent publication lists over 40 learning management systems that are commercially available in the UK. We look at learning management systems in more detail in Chapter 12.

CASE STUDY REVIEW

We shall now review the three hypothetical cases of training development challenges described on pp. 134–35 and consider what role if any e-learning played in meeting them.

CASE STUDY A: MOTOR CAR DEALERSHIP

Solution

Training in customer care for parts department staff will be done by tutor-led face-to-face workshops for groups of 10–12. There is no requirement for electronic learning but both the dealership and the manufacturer would like the workshop scheduling and student attendance and certification recorded electronically. It is decided to run these functions on a learning management system accessible on the manufacturer's intranet.

As regards training in IT the dealership has so far sent people to workshops run by the Chamber Of Commerce. While these are valued, the office manager hopes to offer the option of self-study on PCs in the office to reduce time away from work. The training manager identifies a range of suitable packages on CD-ROM through Learndirect, which staff can run on their desktop machines and/or at home.

Currently car salespeople rely on a combination of sales conferences, newsletters and visits from the regional marketing executive to keep up to date. As this is a problem throughout the dealer network the manufacturer sets up the facility for all dealers to access a 'newsroom' via the manufacturer's learning portal so that all sales staff can keep abreast of developments.

CASE STUDY B: GOVERNMENT DEPARTMENT

Solution

The department designs a learning portal that may be accessed initially from the learning centres. Staff use the portal to profile their learning needs and learning styles, to identify suitable materials and, where it is feasible, to seek accreditation.

The existing authors of the print-based materials receive training in the design of electronic distance learning materials using an authoring system. A web designer is added to the team to adapt existing materials for online delivery and to assist in the production of new online learning programmes.

CASE STUDY C: MEDICAL EQUIPMENT MANUFACTURER

Solution

The company decides to employ a specialist e-learning contractor who uses an authoring system to develop a self-study training programme. They agree to the contractor's suggestion to produce a laminated A4 card to fix by the machine listing the steps of the procedure and key Dos and Don'ts. They are considering the use of a learning management system to record who receives training and when.

Developing your own materials – the THESPIAN case study

We shall review the development of e-learning materials in the context of a hypothetical case within a large organization. An NGO, THESPIAN (The Heritage Special Preservation & Improvement Authority, North) is planning to introduce an appraisal system. The assistant personnel officer managing the project has asked the training development department (TD) to assist in the formulation of a training programme for the new system. They agree a three-strand approach:

- Group sessions facilitated and tutored by volunteer managers. TD will design a tutor support package for use in these sessions.
- A video overview that will explain the aims of the scheme and include two or three cases of typical appraisals and their outcomes.
- An e-learning package that may be studied by individuals or small groups to explain appraisal procedures and how to complete the documentation. This will be delivered on THESPIAN's intranet.

THE DESIGN OF THE PACKAGE

The e-learning package will comprise three modules:

1 Roles and responsibilities
2 The appraisal interview
3 Completing the form

There will be an audio voiceover and several mini cases of appraisal interviews using still photographs (taken mainly from the video) and recorded voices.

RESOURCING THE PROJECT

The TD manager reviews the available resources. They have just completed another project and there are people available within the department to form a development team. A team of four is tasked to design and produce the e-learning package. The roles and responsibilities of the team members are as follows:

- The TD manager is project manager, with responsibilities to:
  - ensure that time targets are achieved
  - work with the author and personnel to ensure that all the content is correct
  - edit the draft materials
  - organize the piloting.
- A courseware designer/author, whose role is to produce a script or storyboard of the modules including all the interactions with users (including questions and feedback).
- A programmer who will convert the storyboards to electronic format.
- A graphic artist to produce photographs and art work and supervise the sound recording.

In estimating the time scale for development the project manager will take into account other tasks to which the various members of the team are committed. It is unlikely that all will be available to work full-time on the project.

THE DEVELOPMENT SCHEDULE

The TD manager draws up a time plan that shows that the development can be completed within 16 weeks. This fits in quite well with personnel's plan to run the tutor-led sessions.

Figure 10.6 is a simplified version of the time plan and allocation of tasks. The sequence is not rigid and could vary between projects. For example instead of defining the learning points for all modules at the start you might decide to do this for each module in turn.

Wk	Activity	PM	AU	PR	GR
1	Draw up specification and modular plan	✓	✓		
2	Interface design	✓		✓	✓
	Learning points for all modules		✓		
3	Storyboard – Module 1		✓		
4					
5	Storyboard – Module 2		✓		
	Coding – Module 1			✓	
	Photos & graphics – Module 1				✓
6					
7	Storyboard – Module 3		✓		
	Record voiceovers				✓
	Coding – Module 2			✓	
	Photos & graphics – Module 2				✓
8					
9	Coding – Module 3			✓	
	Photos & graphics – Module 3				✓
10					
11	Import sound to all modules			✓	
12					
13	Internal edit & revise	✓		✓	
14					
15	Pilot & revise	✓	✓	✓	
16	Release				

(PM = project manager, AU = author, PR = programmer; GR = graphic artist)

Figure 10.6   Time plan for e-learning development

The reader should note that this example exemplifies a schedule for producing a largely stand-alone package for use in a corporate context. The virtual classroom type of learning programme would require a rather different plan that would include setting up a conferencing system, chat room and other features of that particular model.

Since the package is intended to consolidate ground already covered in the group sessions, and tutors are not readily available, it is to be designed for self-study with a high degree of interactivity and testing. Thus in this particular case the work schedule does not include any significant activities involving a tutor, such as preparing briefing notes.

CHECKLIST: DRAWING UP A DEVELOPMENT PLAN

Be sure that you have a competent project manager
Set up all activities in advance
Ensure all involved are aware of their responsibilities
Allow time for the customer to review progress at key stages
Set achievable targets and stick to them
Bear in mind the negative consequences of slippage (for example customer disaffection, fall in staff morale, delays to other projects)
Develop a fall back plan (for example additional programming resources, external suppliers)
Run some tasks in parallel
Re-shooting video and re-recording audio may not be practicable (for example actors unavailable)
Don't skimp on the pilot in an effort to make up lost time

Learning centres and their management

In the first part of this chapter we considered the media for delivering e-learning. A closely related issue is the location for learning. One of the options is a learning centre: a formalized environment for e-learning delivery, separate from both home and the immediate working environment.

In this section we do not purport to provide a definitive guide to learning centres and their management; several publications already do this very well (for example Malone 1997, Department for Education and Employment 2000). But the learning centre is a key feature in many e-learning schemes in both the education and the corporate sectors. An indication of their perceived importance is the award to the learning centre manager of the year at the World Open Learning Conference and Exhibition (WOLCE). Hence the need to cover the topic in this book.

LOCATION OPTIONS

'Where to study?' is a question that confronts most e-learners when they start a learning programme. There are three main options:

- home
- work
- learning centre.

Other options such as 'while commuting' are only available to some or are so uncertain that they cannot be planned for.

In a corporate context studying at one's workplace is seen by many managers as the optimum solution. George and Cooper report that 'all companies favour on-the-job training whether they invest in additional training resources or not' (2001:4) E-learning applications of on-the-job training (desktop learning) began to gain acceptance in business towards the end of the 1990s. In the past three to four years more and more leading companies and government departments have launched online desktop training schemes.

Recent experience seems to suggest that the case for desktop learning may not be so clear-cut. George and Cooper make the point that

> the issue brought up most frequently ... is the difficulty employees found fitting training in around their work. This is an interesting finding as it directly contradicts the benefit that the companies stated the training provided. It high-lights the tension that exists between pressure of work and the need for training and that is not necessarily overcome by the use of flexible learning methods. (2001:3)

It seems that what e-learners prefer does not necessarily match managers' expectations.

Figure 10.7 summarizes the benefits and drawbacks of the three learning environments. It could be argued that there is really little difference between these three options since in every case the learner will be studying online. But this is to ignore a number of significant psychological and pedagogical factors such as the need to socialize, the need for feedback and the importance of a suitable environment for learning that meets the requirements of individuals.

	Advantages	**Disadvantages**
Home	Familiar environment Time flexibility Relaxation Privacy	Distractions Interruptions Lack of face-to-face support Learner pays for internet access
Work	Familiar environment Resources Faster Internet access	Interruptions Limited time flexibility No privacy Limited help available
Learning Centre	Support available Resources Other learners Freedom from interruption Internet access may be faster	Got to get there Time limitations

Figure 10.7   The advantages and disadvantages of three possible locations for e-learning

TYPES OF LEARNING CENTRE

There are many ways of classifying learning centres. One basic division is between private (closed?) centres set up to meet the needs of the employees of a particular organization such as a government department or a large corporation and those that are open to any individual in a particular geographical area. In the latter category centres may run their own programme or they may operate as satellites of a national scheme such as the University for Industry's Learndirect enterprise or the UK Online Network.

CASE STUDY: LEARNDIRECT

The use of the Learndirect centres is a key feature of the UfI's national strategy. It is perceived as the best means of achieving inclusivity in learning by attracting to learning centres many of those for whom schooling was unrewarding. Learndirect guarantees 'that learners will be able to pursue their learning at any Learndirect centre, or from work or home and receive the same level of support in any one centre as in any other'.

Both Learndirect and UK Online centres aim to reflect the inclusivity criterion by locating themselves in easily accessible sites. These include fixed locations such as libraries, Internet cafes, community and leisure centres as well as some mobile centres.

FEATURES OF A LEARNING CENTRE

The features and characteristics of learning centres will vary between organizations, depending on local requirements and available resources. Some will be unstaffed, others will include tutors, administrators and technicians. Some will stock learning programmes and reference materials on a wide range of topics, others will focus on a single subject. Setting up a centre calls for decisions to be made about equipment, facilities for socializing and relaxing, administration and pedagogic support.

In Figure 10.8 we classify the features of the learning centre under these four headings. A centre providing all these elements is likely to found in a larger company or college library, or it may be purpose-designed by a local authority to meet the needs of a local community.

Both the University for Industry's Learndirect network and the DfES's network of UK online centres are national networks each comprising several hundred centres. As we have noted, these centres may be located in a variety of existing host organizations such as libraries, colleges and community centres. To gain Learndirect or UK Online accreditation a centre needs to demonstrate that it provides a range of facilities such as those listed in Figure 10.8, that it will be open at certain times and provide a minimum level of support. Closed learning centres, run by organizations for their own employees, will wish to set standards appropriate to the needs of their learners. If you are responsible for such a centre you may be able to use ideas from the Learndirect centres.

Figure 10.9 is the descriptive web page of the Learndirect centre operated by Park Lane College, Leeds. Note that the centre caters for disabled learners as well as for learners with young children.

THE BENEFITS OF LEARNING CENTRES

A learning centre offers four main benefits over the alternatives:

- It provides a place where learners can study free from interruption.
- It is a repository of learning and reference materials and the means of delivering them that cannot be created at the desktop or at home.

Fixtures and equipment
- Individual study positions
- Delivery system (for example multimedia PCs)
- Internet access
- Video viewing
- Document reproduction facilities (for example printer, scanner, photocopier)

Social items
- Refreshments (for example drinks machine)
- Sitting out area
- Noticeboard
- Pay phone

Administration systems
- Learner enrolment
- Booking system
- Materials inventory

Pedagogical features
- Learning guidance
- Learning materials
- Tutorial support
- Group meeting room
- Assessment system

Figure 10.8   Features of a learning centre

- It usually provides face-to-face support at least in the form of help to get started and basic help with learning skills. some centres may also have subject specialists on hand or available by phone or electronically.
- It provides an opportunity to meet other learners.

These are compelling reasons why the learning centre, as a physical entity, will continue to have value despite the ability to deliver electronically to the desktop at work or home an increasingly wide range of media. However there will be learners who, for a variety of reasons, would value the opportunity to exploit the features of a learning centre but who cannot physically attend a centre. Such learners may be able to study via a so-called virtual learning centre. These learners will use the Internet to access the virtual centre from home or work. Through the virtual centre they can obtain their learner profile, match their needs against available resources, identify a suitable learning programme to meet their needs and, possibly, obtain accreditation. While they are learning they may obtain tutorial guidance and feedback.

---

learndirect centre – full details

Bridge street centre (Access Point)

address: Park Lane College
Leeds Business Centre
Bridge Street
LEEDS
WEST YORKSHIRE
LS2 7QZ

web address:

contact information:

general information: Bridge Street is the location of the Park Lane College 'Leeds Business Centre'. It is located at the lower end of the city centre adjacent to Quarry Hill West Yorkshire Playhouse, Leeds Bus Station and the Eastgate/Vicar Lane areas and Leeds/ Kirkgate Market. The Access Point is located in the Library and Learning Centre on the ground floor of the building with good access and full-time staffing.

facilities: Light refreshments and vending facilities available.

opening hours: Monday–Thursday 08.30–13.00 & 14.00–17.00
Friday 10.00–13.00 & 14.00–16.00

learners with disabilities: Wheelchair access

creche facilities: Awaiting details

contact details

primary phone number:

primary fax number:

primary email address:

contact:

Figure 10.9   Details of a Learndirect centre as available on the Web

MANAGING THE CENTRE

As with all the other elements of the e-learning project the organization will need to establish systems, procedures and documentation for managing the learning centre. Figure 10.10 provides a list of typical management systems.

Resources	How will learning materials be identified and acquired?
Contact and support	How will learners contact centre staff and tutors? How will support be provided?
Use	When will the centre be open? How will learners gain access? What records will be kept of use?
Maintenance	What checks will be made on the condition of the centre? How will remedial work be obtained and monitored?
Technology	How will equipment and systems be specified, recorded and replaced?
Evaluation	How will usage be audited? By what criteria will the centre be judged to have succeeded?
Liaison	How will the centre maintain links with other centres and useful departments within the organization?
Marketing and promotion	By what means will learners and other stakeholders gain information about the centre?

Figure 10.10   Functions for which management systems will be required

STAFFING THE CENTRE

Some centres will be run by a single individual some by a substantial team. In every case three roles will be performed: administrator, tutor and technician (Figure 10.11).

Role	Responsible for
Administrator	Enrolment of new learners Ordering and maintaining learning materials Day-to-day operations Promoting the centre
Tutor	Helping new learners get started Advising on study skills Troubleshooting misunderstandings Giving feedback on assignments Assessment
Technician	Ensuring equipment functions properly Troubleshooting system problems Advice on acquisition of new equipment and systems

Figure 10.11   Roles of staff in a learning centre

SUMMARY

- The choice of media to deliver e-learning programmes must be determined by the learner's need not the technology to be used.
- Different types of learner study more effectively with different media.
- When introducing new methods it is important to win management support.
- The media used to deliver the learning programme must be the most suitable for the practice of the skills described in the learning outcomes.
- Specialist skills are required to develop stand-alone e-learning programmes for online delivery.
- Effective learning can be achieved through computer conferencing systems and e-mail, but some proprietary systems provide significant added value.
- When selecting a learning management system avoid products that are too complex or are incompatible with existing personnel record systems.
- A learning portal facilitates access to corporate e-learning programmes.
- The development of effective e-learning programmes depends upon good project management .
- Because desktop learning is not always desirable a learning centre can be a significant element in the e-learning strategy.
- Learning centre staff must be well-trained and highly motivated.

11 *Managing the E-learning Development Team*

THIS CHAPTER WILL HELP YOU:

- identify the skills needed for e-learning (as opposed to those applicable to more conventional teaching)
- identify the roles you will need to set up an e-learning operation
- define the skill repertoire for all staff working in the e-learning domain
- define criteria for out-sourcing materials development
- manage external suppliers
- set up and manage a personal development plan for e-learning staff.

E-learning is not just another form of lecturing. This is a truism but it seems that all organizations new to e-learning have to learn this lesson for themselves. As we have already pointed out, the most significant difference between e-learning and conventional lecturing is the place of the learner: the learner is at the centre of the programme. This has inevitable implications for the staff designing and delivering e-learning programmes.

Furthermore, e-learning comprises a very specific set of activities:

- the design, production and testing of new learning materials
- the storage of materials
- the despatch of materials
- arranging for learners to access materials (for example in learning centres)
- monitoring learners' progress
- assessing and accrediting learners
- evaluating the e-learning system.

In this chapter we focus mainly on production and development staff (Chapter 8 looks at the role of tutors in helping learners to benefit from the programme).

In organizations with little previous experience of e-learning or related methodologies (such as open and distance learning) the existing lecturing staff (if indeed there are any) are unlikely to have the skills and knowledge required to perform most of these e-learning functions. In some respects an educational institution such as a college or university will actually be at a disadvantage in comparison with a business or government enterprise, since its culture maintains 'lecturing' as an educational paradigm established by centuries of precedent.

E-learning and more conventional approaches to training

In conventional teaching the role of the 'lecturer' or 'trainer' is still paramount. In e-learning this role is taken on by the 'author' (sometimes also referred to as the 'designer' or 'developer' of the programme). The author plans and writes the interactive sequences (lessons) that help learners explore and practise the capabilities they are seeking to acquire. This activity parallels that of the lecturer who explains a new concept or procedure and gives practice in its performance during a well-planned conventional lesson.

A key difference between e-learning and class teaching is that when the distant learner is interacting with the programme the author, unlike the lecturer, is not present to deal with any misunderstandings. This may seem obvious but the implications are not always immediately grasped by the novice developer. Experienced class teachers can go into a classroom with minimum preparation. They deal with learners' misunderstandings, using knowledge acquired from teaching the subject over many years. The author of an e-learning programme must get all that knowledge out of their head and on to paper (or the screen) before they can start writing the lesson. If they are unfamiliar with the subject matter they must persuade an expert to explain it to them. Hence the need for the detailed process of dividing and subdividing the topic to be learned into its component parts, described in Chapter 6. This enables the author to cover the topic thoroughly and to devise questions and problems that explore all the key points that the individual needs to learn.

A good class teacher may make a good author but this is by no means certain. The skill profile is essentially different, as Figure 11.1 demonstrates. When selecting potential developers for an e-learning team you need to address the qualities listed in the second column of the figure.

Teachers . . .	Authors . . .
• think on their feet • talk fluently • are subject-oriented • present topics orally • give a solo performance • manage classes and groups • memorize the learning content	• plan intensively • write fluently • may not necessarily be subject experts • rarely meet learners and thus have less need for well-developed interpersonal skills • tend to be team members • anticipate the needs and difficulties of individual learners • think logically

Figure 11.1   Teachers versus authors

THE RELATIONSHIP BETWEEN CUSTOMER AND PROVIDER

Before we consider the specific roles of the e-learning team it is worth remembering that the design of learning programmes is not a one-way process. There are usually two parties involved: the customer and the provider.

The customer–provider relationship takes many forms. Figure 11.2 gives some examples. Both parties are involved in development. The customer's time commitment will usually be

Customer	Product	Provider
Insurance department of a financial institution	Online package on features and benefits of a new product	In-house development team
Government department	Package on appraisal	External consultants
Leonardo da Vinci programme	Online tutoring	Consortium of small businesses

Figure 11.2   Customer, product and provider

less than that of the provider but, if their needs are to be met, the customer cannot be entirely passive. Figure 11.3 gives one version of the development sequence, showing the respective roles of customer and provider. In this case the customer takes the lead in drawing up the specification for the programme (often this is done in collaboration with the provider). Thereafter the customer is involved in signing off the work done at key stages. This should avoid significant reworking towards the end of programme development. Field testing (piloting) the draft package will certainly involve the customer, who will need to identify the members of the test group and ensure that they can be released from their normal duties to take part in the piloting.

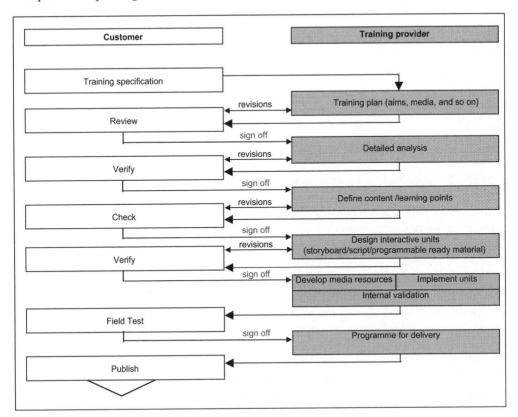

Figure 11.3   Courseware development – cutomer and provider roles

The e-learning development team: roles and skills

ROLES OF TEAM MEMBERS

In some cases all the activities in the training provider column in Figure 11.3 may be undertaken by one person; for example we know of individual university lecturers who have produced online modules to teach particular aspects of their subject. Such a polymath is, though, rare, especially in an occupational training environment, where there tends to be greater time pressure and a tradition of greater role differentiation.

So most e-learning development is carried out by teams. A recent report published by the then Department for Education and Employment (DfEE) surveyed the human resourcing aspects of the e-learning development process in the corporate training context (Arenicola Designs 2000). The report identified six roles that e-learning developers typically undertake. These are defined in Figure 11.4.

Role	Area of responsibility
Project leader	Project management (targets, budget, team); liaison with client and subject experts; installation and maintenance of the package; management of piloting and evaluation
Instructional designer	Content analysis and curriculum design; programme planning; planning and implementation of piloting and evaluation
Courseware designer	Interface and screen design; storyboard/script/programmable ready material
Programmer	Coding; integration with learning management system
Graphics designer	Development and production of graphics and animation
Audio-visual co-ordinator	Sound and video production; still photography

Figure 11.4   Roles of e-learning developers

This is a hypothetical team. Practice varies widely between organizations. Two or more of the six roles in the table may overlap in some smaller teams. The roles of instructional designer and courseware designer are often combined. In other teams a particular area of responsibility may be separately allocated to one person. For example the in-house editing of draft scripts may be the duty of a specific team member rather than one of the many duties of the project leader. Titles also vary widely: the 'instructional designer' may be known as a 'curriculum designer'; the 'courseware designer' is sometimes called the 'author'. Some skills sets remain distinct: instructional design, for example, requires pedagogical skills (such as devising questions and giving feedback) whereas programming requires IT skills (such as database design and coding in an authoring system).

Team size varies from one or two people to (in larger organizations) teams of about eight. In-house teams tend to be smaller (typically three or four members) than specialist providers, who will also probably support a video production resource (in-house teams tend to subcontract this function).

PROJECT MANAGEMENT

When large-scale development projects fail the cause is usually poor project management. This is especially true of projects involving collaboration between several providers. Respondents to the DfEE survey rated project management skills most highly, not only for project leaders but also for instructional designers.

These are the key issues that the project manager should handle:

- time scales (there should be a time plan with milestones, possibly using the critical path technique)
- allocation of roles (at the start the project manager should assign particular staff to the necessary development roles)
- budgetary monitoring
- adherence to quality standards
- liaison with the customer and with subject experts
- definition of stages in development and customer sign-offs
- briefing and management of external contractors.

MANAGING PRINT AND ELECTRONIC MATERIALS DEVELOPMENT

Since the focus of this book is e-learning we do not discuss detailed aspects of the design of printed learning materials. However, from a management perspective there is a decision to be made: whether to separate or integrate the production facilities for printed and electronic learning materials. In some organizations the team producing print-based materials are physically separate from the e-learning group. For many years one government department based its CBT development team in one city and produced printed distance learning materials in another 50 miles away. This tends to produce different cultures and reinforces the fallacious idea that the two sets of processes are completely different. Where possible, you may choose to locate staff within one area, to encourage synergy and allow opportunities for a professional team ethos to develop.

SKILLS REQUIRED FOR E-LEARNING DEVELOPMENT

The DfEE report (Arenicola Designs 2000) identified 40 e-learning development skills, which can be reduced to a dozen key skills:

- project management
- subject matter analysis
- modular sequencing
- writing objectives and tests
- interface design
- writing clearly
- graphic design
- questioning technique
- giving feedback
- using authoring software
- developmental testing
- assessment.

The DfEE researchers recorded the skills that the 100 or so practising designers who responded believed to be priorities for the roles of project leader, instructional designer and courseware designer. Figure 11.5 gives the top ten responses for each role.

Rank	Project leader	Instructional designer	Courseware designer
1	Project management	Instructional design	Interactive screen design
2	Client management	Understanding how people learn	English Language skills
3	Planning	Training techniques	Storyboarding
4	Costing and budgeting	Writing aims and objectives	Assessment techniques
5	English Language skills	English Language skills	Questioning techniques
6	Performance analysis	Task analysis	Understanding how people learn
7	Training needs analysis (TNA)	Training needs analysis (TNA)	Simulation design and development
8	Understanding how people learn	Subject matter research skills	Instructional design
9	Word processing	Questioning techniques	Media selection
10	Evaluation techniques	Assessment techniques	Scriptwriting for audio and video

Figure 11.5   Priority skills for e-learning developers

In-house development versus outsourcing

Should you build up an in-house team or contract out development? This is not an 'all or nothing' decision. As the chart in Figure 11.3 indicates there are many steps in the course development process. Even an organization with an existing, experienced, development team may need to consider commissioning an external source from time to time.

If you are in an exploratory phase, and are not yet committed one way or the other, you need to identify and evaluate the pros and cons carefully. These are reviewed in Figure 11.6. Once you have made your choice you need to think through the implications. Whether you choose the in-house option or contract out there a number of factors to bear in mind.

Factors supporting in-house development	Factors supporting use of a contractor
• You are in direct control • Your staff will enhance their skills • Development over several projects should be cheaper • Maintenance of the product should be easier • You know the company culture • Fewer copyright problems should arise	• A fixed term commitment • No resources to re-allocate after the project • Expertise already available in project management, course design, and so on • Likely to work faster • More aware of recent developments • Not influenced by internal politics • May be more credible than internal developers • Access to latest specialist software

Figure 11.6   In-house development versus outsourcing

THE IN-HOUSE OPTION

These are the points you need to consider if you decide that the work should be done in-house:

- You may need to select and employ one or more people to form your team.
- Staff will probably need training in the design of interactive lessons and in the use of development software, but such training may have a low priority and status in your organization.
- Staff may expect a reasonable time in post and consequent career prospects. (People transferred from a line job into training development may find that, after two years, their old job is no longer available but that there is no future in the e-learning team.)

CONTRACTING OUT

If you choose to contract development outside your organization you may need to consider the following points:

- The more detailed information you can give the contractor the more effective the outcome is likely to be.
- The contractor will need regular assistance from a knowledgeable and reasonably senior person within the organization. This can be a significant unanticipated commitment.
- Changes to the materials after stages have been signed off may be expensive.
- Contractors may find it difficult to pick up procedures in a specialized industry.

If you contract out all the work then you will not need an in-house development team. However, there will still be a need for specialist roles, as shown in Figure 11.7. Often these three roles will be performed by two persons; occasionally by just one. There may also be a steering group that oversees the whole project and to which the project manager reports.

Role	Description
A liaison person	Goes between company and contractor; sets up site visits and meetings with subject matter experts/line managers and so on
A project manager	Monitors that project is on schedule and that outputs are satisfactory; controls budget; chairs project meetings; reports to management
A commissioning editor	Draws up project specification; leads on selection of provider; briefs contractor; edits initial drafts

Figure 11.7   In-house roles

Staff recruitment and selection

In the UK the various forms of distance learning that were the immediate precursors of e-learning go back a generation or more. The industrial training boards, the armed forces and several larger financial institutions began developing alternatives to classroom instruction in the 1960s. The first corporate applications of computer-based training were implemented in 1976. Since that time one might have expected that a new profession of learning materials design and development would have evolved, characterized by a professional body, standards, national examinations leading to accreditation and so forth. This has not been the case. As a result practitioners in the learning technology field generally have low status within their organizations.

Not surprisingly one of the two most difficult roles to fill is that of instructional designer. The other is the project manager.

HOW CAN YOU FIND POTENTIAL STAFF?

There are ten possibilities for finding staff for an e-learning team:

- internal advertising
- external advertising
- national press
- local press
- journals
- the Web
- general recruitment agencies
- specialist recruitment agencies
- membership bodies
- further and higher educational institutions.

Many of these options are denied to training managers in some companies where there is a ban on external recruitment. For those who are permitted to be more adventurous, research suggests that internal advertising and direct recruitment from further and higher education institutions are the most effective options.

SELECTION METHODS

Selection techniques for e-learning staff do not differ greatly from those for many other types of staff. These are the possibilities:

- interviews
- general assessment tests (for example psychometric testing)
- aptitude tests for e-learning related skills
- checking on skills/experience cited on CV
- following up references
- use examples of previous work (a portfolio)

APTITUDE TESTS

In view of the constraints we discussed in the introduction to this section it is not surprising that there are no publicly available packages or exercises tailored to the selection of e-learning developers. However, some larger employers with in-house teams have designed their own aptitude tests. Typically the candidate would be asked to complete tests when they attend for job interview. Tests for an instructional designer, for example, might include:

- questioning skills
- interactive design in learning materials
- logical thinking
- fluency in writing.

The candidate might be asked to tackle a small but discrete design task, for example to produce a one page leaflet on 'How to wire a 3 pin plug', 'How to calculate the Fog Index' or on 'Ohm's Law'.

Training the e-learning team

In this section we address the question of training production and development staff – from the point of view of the e-learning manager within business or government.

Whatever form the in-house team takes, and whatever the job titles it employs, the skills that are required will be the same. The skills identified earlier can be sorted into four groups, as in Figure 11.8.

When the in-house team is first set up there is likely to be an imbalance in the distribution of these skills. Both graphic design and IT are subjects in which qualified practitioners abound; the topics feature among the most popular courses in further and higher education institutions. Thus the e-learning team members responsible for programming and graphic design may be expected to possess most of the skills necessary to make an immediate contribution to the programme. If it is decided to recruit a new programmer or graphic artist from outside the company, the job description and qualifications are fairly easy to specify. Subsequent training is likely to take the form of updating on new software packages.

Skill group	Examples
Pedagogical skills	Designing interactive modules, defining outcomes, devising questions and problems, giving feedback
IT skills	Coding using authoring software, using special purpose design tools (for example for animations)
Project management	Work scheduling, budgeting, client management
Graphic design	Using graphic design software, using special purpose graphics tools to incorporate audio-visual material

Figure 11.8   Four main skills groups for developing materials

On the other hand, those assigned the roles of project leader and author/designer are far less likely to have received any formal training in the required skills. They are often recruited internally. In a bank, for example, instructional designers may be transferred from branch banking to the training department for, say, two years. They may have no previous experience as trainers.

One question investigated by the DfEE survey was 'What e-learning development skills are in short supply?' The top four were:

- understanding how people learn
- project management
- training needs analysis
- evaluation.

Instructional design followed closely behind. The likelihood is that all these skills will need to be learned from scratch.

SOURCES AND TYPES OF TRAINING

Few systematic courses are available in topics related to e-learning design, at least in the UK. The situation in North America is quite different: many institutions in Canada and the USA offer learning programmes in learning design up to post-graduate level. Options that exist from UK providers are summarized in Figure 11.9.

Figure 11.10 describes three examples of training programmes for e-learning practitioners:

- a diploma/degree course (ALT)
- a shorter accredited course (LeTTOL)
- a workshop.

Type of training	Duration	Format
Diploma/degree courses	2 years	Traditional class taught full-time and part-time Distance learning with occasional group meetings
Shorter accredited courses (for example leading to a certificate or credits)	13 weeks	Online
Workshops	3–10 days	Lecture-demonstrations, individual activities, project work in small groups
Self-study packages	1–3 hours	CD-ROM or web-delivered
Special courseware development tools	ongoing	Performance support software including training
On-the-job	ongoing	Assignment based, mentoring by line manager/peers

Figure 11.9   Options for training staff for e-learning

Title and Provider	Duration	Content and structure	Qualification
ALT Programme (Advanced learning technology) Lancaster University	30–48 months	The design, production, use and evaluation of IT-based learning resources. The structure is modular (six modules), designed for part-time study, combining independent study with short residential periods. Tutorial support via computer-managed conferencing. Participants can start the programme at any one of three points in the year.	Postgraduate Diploma/MSc MSC
LeTTOL (Learning to teach on-line) SYFEC (South Yorkshire Further Education Consortium)	18–20 weeks	Teaching and supporting learners online; use of the Internet as a resource; design of online materials.	Open College credits at Level 4
The design of technology-based training Peak Dean Interactive Limited	5 days	The analysis, planning, design and production of e-learning courseware for occupational trainers. Combination of lecture-demonstration, individual and group project work and e-learning modules.	Certificate of attendance

Figure 11.10   Examples of e-learning training opportunities

SUMMARY

- Agree the development methodology to be used (see Chapters 1, 2, 4, 5, 6).
- Define standards for courseware (see Chapters 10 and 12).
- Select projects to develop.
- Decide whether to develop the programme in-house or via outsourcing.
- If in-house, identify team roles.
- Select team members.
- Train designers in curriculum planning and developing interactive learning.
- Train coders/programmers in the use of development software.
- Define the 'tutor' role (see Chapter 8).
- Select tutors (see Chapter 8).
- Train tutors (see Chapter 8).

12 *Learning Management Systems and Standards*

THIS CHAPTER WILL HELP YOU:

- define the characteristics of learning management systems that support both classroom training and online learning
- define the functions of a managed learning environment
- define the benefits offered by a learning management system
- define criteria for selecting a learning management system
- explain why standards are important in the learning technology field
- define 'learning objects' and 'metadata'
- list key actors in the standards field

This chapter deals with two closely related topics: learning management systems and learning technology standards. These are by their very nature fairly technical. However, sooner or later they will affect the work of most trainers and educators working in the e-learning field and many who use more conventional training methods.

In discussing both topics we shall use a large number of technical terms and acronyms. We'll do our best to explain these as we go and many can also be found in the glossary at the end of the text.

What is a learning management system?

A recent report from the Department for Education & Skills (DfES) describes a learning management system (LMS) as 'a software package that supports the management of learning in an organisation' (Dean 2001). Reading this many will ask themselves what is the difference between a learning management system and the computer managed learning (CML) systems that have been around for 30 years or so. The short answer is 'in most cases, very little'. Learning management systems are the next stage in the evolution of CML systems.

FEATURES OF A LEARNING MANAGEMENT SYSTEM

The DfEE report describes four types of features provided by different types of learning management system. These are:

- standard features, to be found in any LMS

- features special to classroom training
- features that support distance learning off-line
- features required for online learning.

Standard features of an LMS

As we have noted, computer managed learning systems have been available for many years. These provide basic information about learners' progress, for both the learners themselves and for their sponsors. They also provide information about the use of the programme for the administrator. These standard features generally include:

- learner registration data (personal details, user name, password, and so on)
- programme registration data (prerequisites, qualifications, average study times)
- learner progress data (completed modules, test results, and so on).

CASE STUDY: LMS AT UNIVERSITY OF SHEFFIELD

An example of the use of a LMS in an HE context is the Canadian package WebCT, as used in the Department of Biomedical Science at the University of Sheffield in the teaching of one course on human histology and another on pregnancy. The histology course is currently available to 270 students via the Department's Web page.

WebCT enables the course manager to keep close track of learners' progress by means of online quizzes and an end of course quiz. Figure 12.1 reports how one learner performed on the end of course quiz; Figure 12.2 is an example of a summary of the performance of a group of learners.

Features that support classroom learning

An LMS that can administer classroom learning will be used particularly in allocating resources, such as space and equipment. The functions it will include are:

- timetabling of rooms
- allocation of trainers
- booking of supporting equipment – video projectors, PCs
- timetabling of learners
- reporting, including timetables, joining instructions, and so on.

Features that support off-line distance learning

These features will be present in an LMS used to manage and support off-line distance learning and will incorporate a variety of media from print to CD-ROM. An LMS that supports off-line distance learning is also likely to include a function for allocating tutors to learners. This kind of function tended not to feature in CML systems that accompanied CBT authoring software.

Features that support online learning

Of most interest to readers of this book are likely to be learning management systems that

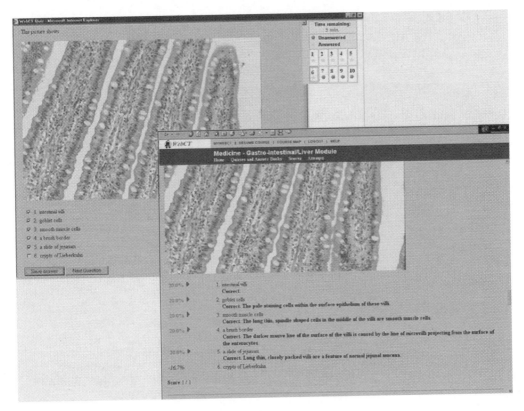

Figure 12.1   Individual feedback in an online quiz

can support online learning. The DfES report points out that these tend to be quite complex. In addition to the basic features they may also support:

- online delivery of technology-based training (TBT)
- courseware development
- methods of charging users and paying providers
- online conferencing with peers and tutors
- bookmarking so that learners returning to a lesson can restart where they left off
- online tutorial support
- downloading of support materials for printing or for studying off-line.

Additional features

Some learning management systems include more advanced functionality designed to help staff and their managers diagnose training needs and plan solutions, for example:

- recommending courses based on an employee's profile and experience
- devising training plans for staff who are moving within the company
- identifying trends (for example a need in the company for greater knowledge of e-commerce)
- identifying resource implications (for example the need for platforms with greater bandwidth).

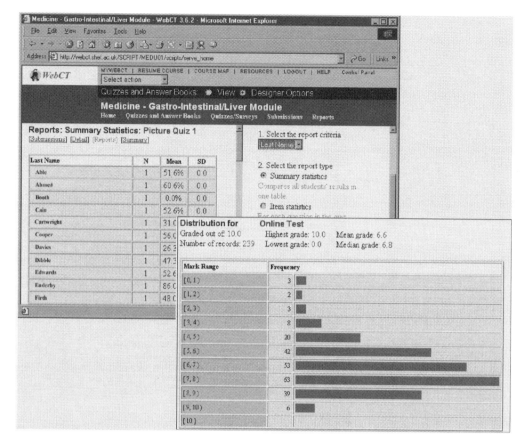

Figure 12.2   Summative assessment for a group

Managed learning environments

'Managed learning environment' is a term used to describe a software system that incorporates all the functions described above. It can be seen as the third stage on a continuum that begins with CML and passes through LMS (Figure 12.3).

| CML | LEARNING MANAGEMENT | MANAGED LEARNING |
| SYSTEM | SYSTEM | ENVIRONMENT |

Figure 12.3   The continuum of learning management

The expression 'managed learning environment' is not mentioned in the recent DfES report that we cited. A Higher Education Funding Council for England (HEFCE) report defines a Managed Learning Environment as

> a complete integrated system needed to support on-line learning. This includes not
> only the learning management system used for teaching and learning but also the

supporting administrative systems, student records, finance, course catalogues, student services and others.

(Dean et al. 2000:1)

As is so often the case there is a blurring between the definitions of learning management system and managed learning environment. The HEFCE report attempts to clarify the distinction by dividing the functionality of a managed learning environment into two categories – learning management functions and administrative and financial functions (Figure 12.4).

Learning management functions	Content delivery, authoring, sequencing, metadata, course preparation, collaboration, questioning and testing
Administrative and financial functions	E-commerce, enrolment, student fees, student profiling, student records, course catalogues, employer enquiries

Figure 12.4   Functionality in a managed learning environment

In a managed learning environment the three principal parties to the e-learning process – the learner, tutor and course administrator – will access the facilities listed in Figure 12.5.

Learner	**Tutor**	**Administrator**
Noticeboard	Adding and amending course	Student and staff registration
Course outline	modules and assignments	System performance statistics
E-mail	Student grouping	Security
Conferencing tools	Progress recording	Reporting
Class list and student homepages	Marking	Billing and accounts
Assignments and assessments	Course/class statistics	Management information
Synchronous collaboration tools	Communicating with students	Employer queries
Multimedia resources	and groups	
File download		
Support for off-line working		
Calendar		
Search tools		
Bookmarking		
Navigation model		

Figure 12.5   Who gets what in managed learning environments

In Figure 12.6 we can see how a course tutor or administrator can use the noticeboard feature of an LMS for course management. Figure 12.7 is a page from a learner's personal study management diary.

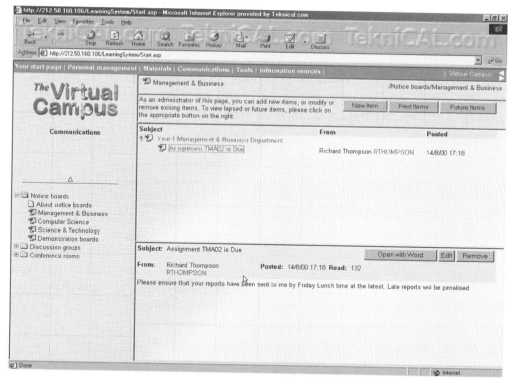

Figure 12.6 Noticeboard message from an online programme

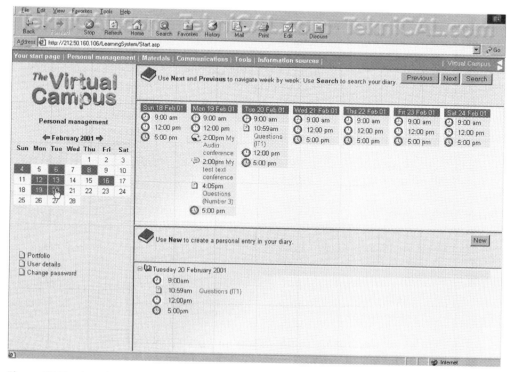

Figure 12.7 An online learner's personal planner

Now we would like to consider why learning management systems are an important, indeed indispensable, piece in the e-learning jigsaw.

The benefits of learning management systems

A learning management system can be a powerful tool for both educational and administrative purposes. As Figure 12.8 shows a learning management system can benefit all the stakeholders in the e-learning process.

User	Application
Course administrators	Registering learners on courses Recording fee payments Scheduling resources
Course designers	Course design templates Questions and tests
Tutors	Monitoring learner progress Communicating with learners
Learning centre managers	Monitoring use of courseware Delivering materials from different suppliers
Learners	Planning learning Taking tests Accreditation Communicating with peers Feedback from tutors

Figure 12.8   Who benefits from a learning management system?

Course designers, tutors and others responsible for the educational effectiveness of learning materials can use the LMS in planning, delivering and evaluating learning. Course administrators may use the system for anything from recording payments of fees to scheduling the use of resources. But most importantly a learning management system can promote the central role of the learner.

Figure 12.9 illustrates the tutor–learner relationship within the conventional teacher-centred model of teaching and learning. This model shows the largely one-way transmission of information by the teacher, typically via a lecture. For most of the time the learners are passive receivers of the words and activities of the teacher. Some forms of e-learning adopt this model. They simply use technology to transmit information more efficiently and in greater quantities than was possible by traditional methods.

Figure 12.10 depicts what has been called the learner-centric model for which e-learning should be the optimum tool. From the diagram we can see that learners may access a kaleido-

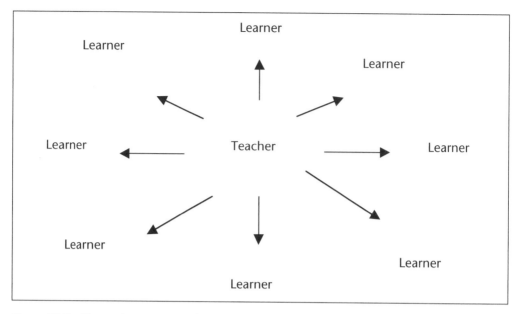

Figure 12.9   The teacher-centric model

scope of resources, many of which – such as e-mail and computer conferencing – are inherently interactive. Of course, since the 1950s – before computers became widely available – there have been examples of imaginative learning systems that have incorporated this kind of approach to enrich the learning process. A learning management system enables these possibilities to become available to far more learners in widely dispersed locations. It can exploit the power of computer networks to allow distant learners to communicate with tutors and with each other.

The learner-centric model of e-learning puts greater emphasis on learner choice. A learning management system maximizes opportunities for learners to choose. The system may make available:

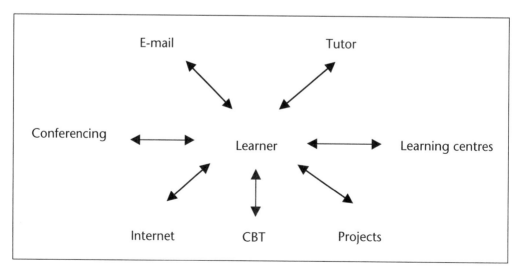

Figure 12.10   The learner-centric model

- resources to help learners start at an appropriate point (for example diagnostic tests)
- information on who is available to help and how to contact them
- a record of progress and how to proceed
- tests, exercises, and so on to check and extend learning
- ideas on resources to consult.

One factor that assists this process is what has come to be known as granularity – the breaking down of learning into 'bite-sized chunks'. This is particularly helpful for occupational training applications when learners may only have small windows of opportunity to study.

To use these functions to the full organizations need to be learner-centred: this is our argument throughout this book. As we shall see there are also additional organizational and administrative benefits for the organization itself.

The collaborative environment

Earlier we cited the definition of a learning management system as 'a software package'. While this is true it is also worth pointing out that in a larger organization, such as a university, the LMS will often reside within a particular hardware configuration. This too will have the aim of enabling the effective administration of an educational system.

One term used to describe this hardware/software integration is the 'collaborative environment'. An article in the US publication *Government Computer News* describes a collaborative environment as a system that supports e-mail, videoconferencing and web hosting as well as portable group computing platforms, which combine Internet, TV and personal computing.

CASE STUDY: ROTHERHAM CITY LEARNING CENTRE

An example of a collaborative environment that has been installed in the UK is the Rotherham City Learning Centre (CLC). This is one of the first of a national network of learning centres established towards the end of 2000 by the UK government under its Excellence in Cities programme. The CLC environment connects together schools in Rotherham as one large flat network that runs at Ethernet speed 100Mbs. These connections are made at a hub which is the Wide Area Network (WAN) centre at the Rotherham Civic Building. Internet access is by a link from the WAN Centre direct to the London Internet Exchange (LINX).

There is provision at this centre for conferencing, e-mail and web hosting in addition to other standard Internet services. The idea is that schools can receive these services over high speed links rather than the traditional 'narrow band' wide area links such as ISDN. The CLC's website claims that the project involves creating a curriculum of on-line learning materials that will provide valuable distance learning opportunities. Different strands of learning content will act as shared resources promoting collaborative learning and extending the range of learning opportunity that is available to each pupil.

As we have noted above, a Learning Management System is the term currently used for what used to be called computer managed learning. We have already mentioned such administrative functions as registering students on courses, achievement testing, course usage and study times. We should also draw attention to one question that those contemplating investing in a Learning Management System will need to investigate. This is the extent to which the LMS integrates with or links to an authoring system for computer-assisted learning. The proportion of e-learning materials that are web-delivered rather than on CD-ROM has grown exponentially. Browser-based learning materials are usually coded in HTML or Java, which are programming languages for creating web-delivered communications. However, as long as CD-ROM continues to have a use, CBT authoring systems such as Authorware and ToolBook will remain a necessary component of the e-developer's toolbox.

Choosing a learning management system

It is important to get your choice right first time. To do this you first need to define the functions you need for learners in your own context. You will need to be clear about any systems parameters, for example:

- Do you need to transfer data from existing human resource software?
- Do you need to run courseware from different vendors?
- How will the system be costed, for example by usage or on a fixed cost basis?
- What is the likely throughput of learners?

Other factors crucial to making the right choice include:

- a clear specification
- early and good liaison with the IT department
- a plan to train staff to support the LMS.

Standards in e-learning

The connection between a Learning Management System and standards may not be immediately obvious. However, as we shall show they are closely connected. To give one example: we explain later that one important requirement for users of learning technology products concerns the need to run software from different vendors. To achieve this aim standards are necessary so that different publishers produce packages that, whatever their source, have certain basic common characteristics. The learning management system will be designed to support these standards and to run the products – regardless of the software in which they were developed – on the same platform.

First we shall attempt to define what we mean by standards in the context of e-learning generally and learning management systems in particular. Then we shall describe some of the characteristics of standards that course developers, learning centre managers and other practitioners need to take into account. In the process we shall also need to review who are the leading bodies in the drive to establish internationally accepted standards for learning technology.

Like so many terms in education and training the word 'standards' means different things to different people. For instance in the human resources domain occupational standards define the performance requirements for particular employment categories. In learning technology standards help materials designers to produce good quality courseware that is visually appealing, offers learners options for study, is easy to use and achieves its objectives.

STANDARDS AND INTEROPERABILITY

The standards that concern us here are those designed to provide users of learning technology products with maximum flexibility, for example so that they can use the products of different suppliers on the same platform. This leads to greater flexibility and ease of use for learners. The problem that the current standards debates are seeking to resolve has been described by the Aviation Industry CBT Committee (AICC):

> In the past authoring systems made the CBT customer a captive of the authoring system vendors. If the customer wanted to take advantage of the CMI features in courses they had two choices: design their own CMI system (or LMS) or purchase a CMI system from the same vendor. In either case the resulting CMI system works only for a single vendor's CBT lessons. This is fine until the customer acquires CBT courseware designed for a different authoring system.
>
> (www.hq.nasa.gov/office/codeft/AICC-SCORM-standards)

Because CBT systems are proprietary each producer has their own programming, logic codes and so forth. The solution to this problem is one of the key buzzwords of the standards vocabulary – 'interoperability'. Interoperability means that an organization can exploit data from different providers. Interoperability can apply to CBT courseware, curriculum files and student information.

Standards enable interoperability to be delivered by the company's learning management system. Indeed suppliers are increasingly designing learning management systems to meet international standards. Thus, in future, courseware will be produced in accordance with internationally agreed specifications to ensure that content and data from different sources can be exchanged between different end users. An article by Joanne Childs in *t* magazine in June 2000 explained how this will benefit the organization:

> E-learning makes knowledge management possible because the learning management system that distributes the learning materials online from a central server can also gather information about both the usage and the users of that information. It can tell for example which people in an organisation have studied which learning materials, what level of competence they have reached and measure this against the knowledge and skills they need to be competent in their current and future job. This can help an organisation build competency specifications for jobs and employees. Learning Management Systems can launch and monitor any piece of CBT authored in any software.

This last statement emphasizes the link between learning management systems and learning technology standards. With standards in place a company can purchase a single learning management system that can deliver content from any commercial supplier.

Key areas for standards

There are a half-dozen key areas of learning design and development that the learning standards bodies are prioritizing with a view to achieving greater interoperability within e-learning applications. These are:

- descriptors of learning materials (that is learning object metadata)
- taxonomies and vocabularies
- testing, quizzes and questions
- learner profiling
- granularity – the way course content is divided and subdivided
- multilinguality.

Learning objects and metadata

In order to achieve maximum availability and reusability, learning materials must be recorded and described in a uniform way. An analogy to what is happening in the field of learning technology standards is technical abstracting. If you want to research the area of, say, 'Web-based training for the older learner' you can find items relevant to your search listed in a printed or electronic compendium such as ERIC (Educational Resources Information Centre). You might begin your enquiry by searching on keywords or descriptors. In this case you might try WBT, OLDER LEARNER, ADULTS, E-LEARNING and ONLINE LEARNING. The materials that the system identifies might be journal articles, newspaper reports, videos or CD-ROMs but in every case they will be described in the same way. All will have details such as author's name, publisher, date, media type and so forth together with a description of the content – the abstract itself – listed and presented in the same sequence and format. These are so-called metadata or data about data. In the learning technology field the term is found with increasing frequency in the phrase 'learning object metadata' which gives us the inelegant acronym LOM. Learning objects are the e-learning equivalent of the journal articles described by the metadata in a technical abstracting system. A learning object could be a case study, a teaching unit, an illustration or a test.

GRANULARITY

The CEN/ISSS standardization work programme for *Learning & Training Technologies & Educational Multimedia Software* (CEN/ISSS 2000) discusses one way of organizing the learning objects that comprise multimedia content within a learning technology system. This is summarized in Figure 12.11.

Level 0: Atoms – separate items of data, for example a piece of text, a video clip
Level 1: Content units – self-contained learning resource not sensibly divisible
Level 2: Composite units – groupings of content units including navigation
Level 3: Courses – the largest level of granularity representing composite learning experiences, often connected with accreditation

---

Figure 12.11   Levels of learning objects

We demonstrated an example of granularity in the design of learning programmes earlier in Figure 1.10, p. 13.

As the CEN/ISSS report points out, the definition of a learning object is not completely clear and the standards bodies have identified the need to clarify and define a standard for a learning object.

Learning resources metadata is one of four draft standards or specifications that are currently under review. The others are the question and test interoperability specification, the content packaging specification and the enterprise specification.

Who is working on standards?

Dozens of bodies worldwide are seeking to define learning technology standards. The leading participants are the AICC, the Institute for Electrical and Electronic Engineering (IEEE) and the IMS Global Learning Consortium. In the summer of 2000 they came together under the aegis of the Advanced Distributed Learning consortium (ADL), an initiative of the US Department of Defense.

The culmination of their efforts will be a specification currently being agreed by the Learning Technology Standards Committee of the IEEE, commonly referred to as the 'I triple E'. The IEEE will then pass this to ISO, the ultimate authority for conferring standards.

STANDARDS AND COURSE DESIGN

What will the introduction of international standards for learning technology mean to practising course designers? Increasingly people are using the term 'compliant' as in 'Is your courseware IMS (or AICC) compliant?' – meaning 'Does it comply with IMS (or other) international standards?' The implication is that if your materials are non-compliant and don't include metadata and other standard descriptors they will be worthless outside your organization. The reality is less clear-cut. In the UK many organizations that pay lip service to being standards compliant publish materials that pay little, if any, regard to the emerging standards. When an international standard for learning technology is eventually approved, it seems likely that the standards bodies will be faced with a significant challenge to inform and update e-learning users and practitioners as to what they need to do to achieve compliance.

A DEVELOPER'S TOOL

One practical problem has been the lack of guidance and easy-to-use tools on getting started. The ADL has begun to address this issue. The members of ADL include representatives of the US armed forces (who are funding the project) and many of the larger players in the standards arena. ADL has devised a set of tools called SCORM (Shareable Courseware Object Reference Model). SCORM 'will allow courseware designers to update and recycle courses by inserting new information and easily removing outdated material. Databases throughout the learning management system will allow administrators to track, list and manage student progress over the Internet.' This in turn 'will allow the Navy, Air Force, Army and Marines to exchange training content and data, no matter which vendor it came from' <www.adlnet.org>.

In September 2000 the US Army announced a $600 million contract to develop a web portal for online training. To win this contract potential developers must use the SCORM specification as a guideline.

One of the SCORM tools (downloadable from the Web) is a metadata generator – in effect a template that prompts developers to enter the data needed for compliance with the standards. Figure 12.12 contains an extract from that template.

The SCORM tool creates an XML (extensible mark-up language) file. XML is software that has the flexibility to be used on a variety of platforms and thus assists in the achievement of interoperability.

Conclusions

We have reviewed above the criteria for organizations intending to purchase a learning management system. Any organization facing this choice must take into account the provision that the LMS under consideration makes for learning technology standards. Indeed intending purchasers should ask vendors to clarify their plans for standards conformance. Some systems already have AICC certification and this guarantees a minimum level of interoperability between courseware and learning management systems. At the time of writing the standards, while taking shape, are still to be finally agreed. One US developer is reported to be taking a conservative approach by creating HTML-based courseware that can easily be adapted to whatever the standard becomes. This may be a sensible strategy for others to follow until the picture becomes clearer.

SUMMARY

• •

- Any organization implementing an e-learning scheme will benefit by using a learning management system.
- Learning management systems can include administrative, financial, logistical and academic functions.
- If required an LMS can manage both classroom training and distance learning.
- An LMS may support courseware development as well as management functions.
- Before committing yourself to purchase an LMS you must draw up a detailed specification.
- An effective LMS needs to be able to deliver courseware from different sources – this is interoperability.
- International standards for the design, development and delivery of learning materials are being specified currently in order to facilitate interoperability between systems.
- Virtually all practitioners in the e-learning field will need to use or understand learning object metadata.

---

3. Metadata	
3.4 Metadata Scheme:	[ ]
4. Technical	
4.1 Format:	[ ]
4.2 Size:	[ ]
4.3 Location:	[ ]
4.4 Requirements	
4.4.1 Type:	[▼]
4.4.2 Name:	[User_Defined ▼]
4.4.3 Minimum Version:	[ ]
4.4.4 Maximum Version:	[ ]
4.5 Installation Remarks:	[ ]
4.6 Other Platform Requirements:	[ ]
4.7 Duration:	[ ]

Figure 12.12   Extract from SCORM content metadata generator

Glossary

Italicized words feature as separate headings in the glossary.

Accreditation – the process of allocating credit for a *programme* (for example a qualification or points towards a qualification).

Assessment – the process of measuring learner performance. See also *Diagnostic assessment, Formative assessment, Summative assessment*.

Asynchronous learning – electronically mediated communication in which there is a delay between the sending and receipt of messages. See also *Synchronous learning*.

Authoring language/system – software facilitating the preparation of *learning material*.

CBT – computer-based training; learning delivered via the computer, often in a corporate context. The phrase usually implies the presentation of self-paced interactive training on a computer screen, sometimes with some element of learning management. See *CMI/CML*.

CMI/CML – computer-managed instruction/learning; sometimes used synonymously with *computer-based training* but more specifically implying the use of the computer to manage learning, for example by helping the *learner* choose routes through a *programme* and/or recording assessment results for individuals or groups of learners. The outputs of CML include statistical reports of learner performance or system utilization.

Computer conferencing – a dialogue between two or more users in multiple locations in text and/or audio and/or visual mode, managed electronically.

Content analysis – a key stage in the design of the curriculum for a *programme*, entailing the division and sub-division of a topic or skills into logically related components.

Delivery – the means by which *programme* components (such as the *learning material* and any associated *support*) reach learners.

Design – stage in developing an e-learning *programme* that includes the analysis of learner needs and content, leading to decisions on structure, length and *media*, informed by knowledge of the resources available.

Development – this stage in developing an e-learning *programme* follows from the *design* stage; it includes the specification of the three main components of most programmes: *learning material, support,* and management.

Developmental testing – trying out of *learning material* (and other arrangements such as learning management) in draft or prototype version using a small group of learners from the target population (see also *piloting*). The purpose of such testing is to identify improvements that might be made before the *programme* is finalized.

Diagnostic assessment – similar to *formative assessment* but taking place before the *programme* or *module* (for example via a pre-entry test).

EPSS (Electronic Performance Support System) – software providing a variety of support to the desk top; the support could include training, guidance, job aids and information.

Evaluation – the process of reviewing the effectiveness and worth of the *programme*. Evaluation can cover a number of different aspects of the *programme*, including the learning design, value as perceived by the learners, and cost-effectiveness. Evaluation is an occasional rather than continuous process and not necessarily focused on making immediate changes to the operation of the *programme* (in contrast with *monitoring*).

Formative assessment – assessment that takes place as the learner works through the *programme*. The focus of formative assessment is to help individuals learn more effectively by *monitoring* their progress, identifying difficulties and suggesting solutions. Hence the importance of feedback in the process. See also *Assessment, Diagnostic assessment, Summative assessment.*

Goal analysis – a form of training needs analysis designed to translate general aims into specific performance *outcomes.*

Granularity – the way in which a learning *programme* may be divided and sub-divided into smaller sections to provide more flexibility in sequencing and shorter sequences of study. A common approach is to divide programmes into modules and modules into units. See also *Module* and *Section.*

IIP (Investors In People) – the UK national standard for human resources development, which comprises 24 specific component standards.

Learndirect – the brand name of the University for Industry (UfI) through which learning opportunities are provided.

Learner(s) – the group or groups of individuals for whom a *programme* is designed; we use 'learner' as a generic term to cover trainee, employee and student.

Learning centre – a purpose-designed location where learners can access materials and receive *support.*

Learning environment – the context in which a *learner*/learners undertake their activities; an environment has a physical dimension (for example equipment and books) and a virtual dimension (for example networks, other learners/*tutors* not physically present).

Learning Management System (LMS) – software performing a range of administrative and pedagogical functions including registering learners, administering tests, tracking *learner* progress, analysing test performance and facilitating communication between learners and their peers and *tutors.*

Learning material – content of the *programme*; may be in a variety of *media*, for example electronic, print, video or audio

Learning object metadata (LOM) – a method of recording *learning material* using special descriptors.

Learning outcome – a statement of what the *learner* should know/be able to do at the end of a *section, module* or *programme.*

Learning portal – a point of access to an online learning system via a browser. Facilities may include access to a corporate university, internal courses and discussion groups.

Learner profile – the attributes of an individual *learner*, or group of learners, covering, for example, knowledge and skills, cultural background and learning styles.

Learning technology standards – commonly observed specifications for the development of learning programmes covering such areas as content, questions and *learner profiles.*

Managed learning environment – an electronic system combining course administration and management functions with pedagogic functions

Media – means by which *programme* content and *support* reach the *learner* (for example electronic, print, face-to-face, telephone).

Mentor – a rather general term to describe someone who helps the *learner*. Whereas a *tutor*

usually provides specialist help (for example in learning a particular subject or acquiring a particular skill) a mentor is usually supportive in a more general way relevant to their own experience. A mentor might, for example, help the learner set up projects in a workplace with which the mentor is familiar.

Module – self-contained sub-division of a *programme*; modules may also be divided into *sections* or units.

Monitoring – the scrutiny of the day-to-day operation of the *programme* with the aim of making any necessary and immediate changes.

Outcome – see *Learning outcome*.

Performance analysis – a systematic way of identifying the barriers to poor performance within an organization; these may exist at the level of individuals or groups. Performance can be affected by factors relating to people (for example motivation) or to systems and equipment.

Piloting – testing all or part of a *programme* on *learners* from the *target audience*, with a view to making changes before full implementation. (See also *Developmental testing*).

Platform – the hardware/software configuration necessary to deliver electronic learning systems.

Programme – a planned learning experience of any type, length or complexity.

Section – term used in this book to describe the smallest sequence of learning within a *module*; sometimes also known as a 'unit'.

Stakeholder(s) – a group (or groups) with an interest in the *programme* (for example employers).

Summative assessment – assessment that measures the extent to which the learner has achieved the outcomes of the *programme*, often associated with the award of a certificate or credit. See also *Assessment, Diagnostic assessment, Formative assessment*.

Support/learner support – help provided to learners in a *programme* additional to the *learning material* (for example guidance, feedback on their work).

Synchronous learning – electronically-mediated communication carried out in real time. See also *Asynchronous learning*.

Target audience – the group or groups of *learners* at whom the *programme* is aimed.

Tutor – the person professionally responsible for helping individuals or groups to learn in an e-learning scheme. Tutors will often provide specialist help, based on their own expertise in a particular subject area or skill.

UK Online – a network of *learning centres* equipped with information and communications technology, managed by the UK Department for Education and Skills (DfES).

Unit – see *Section*.

References

Arenicola Designs (2000), *Authoring for CBT and Interactive Multimedia*, Department for Education and Employment (DfEE).

Arenson, W. (1998), 'N.Y.U. sees profits in virtual classes', *New York Times*, 7 October: A20.

Bartolic-Zlomislic, S. and Bates A.W. (n.d.), *Investing in Online Learning: Potential Benefits and Limitations* <http://bates.cstudies.ubc.ca/investing.html>.

Bloom, B.S. *et al.* (1964), *Taxonomy of Educational Objectives: Handbook 1: Cognitive Domain*, London: Longmans.

Bourne, John R. *et al.* (1997) 'Paradigms for on-line learning: a case study in the design and implementation of an Asynchronous Learning Networks (ALN) course', *Journal of Asynchronous Learning Networks*, 1(2), <www.aln.org/alnweb/journal/issue2/assee.htm>.

CEN/ISSS (2000), Report CWA14040, October, Brussels. CEN.

Childs, J. (2000), 'The future for e-learning', June, <www.tmag.co.uk>.

Cohen, E. Nigel (1994), *The Business Plan – Approved!* Aldershot: Gower.

Dean, C. (2001), *Technology Based Training and Online Learning*, DfEE, ref: LLTD5 2000.

Dean, C. *et al.* (2000), 'Expert survey of e-tools for the e-university – Electronic Administrative Systems', HEFCE report.

Department for Education and Employment (DfEE) (2000), *Learning Centres: A Guide*, DfEE.

Department of Trade and Industry (DTI) (2000), *The Future of Corporate Learning*, DTI/Pub 4849.

Dowsing, R.D., Long, S. and Craven, P. (2000), *The Effectiveness of Computer-aided Assessment of IT Skills*, International Conference on Learning with Technology (ICLT), Temple University, Philadelphia.

George, A. and Cooper, C. (2001), *Employers' Use and Awareness of Vocational Learning Approaches*, Department for Education and Employment Research Report RB246.

Harless, J. (1975), *An Ounce of Analysis is Worth a Pound of Objectives*, Guild V Publications.

Henley Management College (2000), *Corporate Universities – Learning Partnerships for the Future*, Henley-on-Thames: Henley Management College.

Hiscock, J. (2000), 'Forensics follow e-learning trail', *IT Training*, October.

Malone, Samuel A. (1997), *How to Set Up and Manage a Corporate Learning Centre*, Aldershot: Gower.

Shorrock, T. (2001), 'The e-ssence of e-learning', *Open Learning Today*, January.

Small Firms Enterprise Development Initiative (SFEDI) (2000), *Starting a Successful business*, Department of Trade and Industry (DTI).

Whalen, T. and Wright, D. (2000), *The Business Case for Web Based Training*, Bell, Canada.

Wilson, D. (2000), 'The pitfalls of buying e-learning', *IT Training*, August.

OTHER USEFUL SOURCES

Freeman, R. (1997), *Managing Open Systems,* London: Kogan Page.
Salmon, G. (2000), *E-moderating,* London: Kogan Page.
<http://www.onlinelearningmag.com/current/index.htm>

Index